Guest-edited by
Matias del Campo
and Neil Leach

ARCHITECTURE
AND ARTIFICIAL
INTELLIGENCE

MACHINE
HALLUCINATIONS

03 | Vol 92 | 2022

ISSN 0003-8504   ISBN 978 1119 748847

Guest-edited by **Matias del Campo and Neil Leach**

Editorial Offices
John Wiley & Sons
9600 Garsington Road
Oxford
OX4 2DQ

T +44 (0)18 6577 6868

Editor
Neil Spiller

Managing Editor
Caroline Ellerby
Caroline Ellerby Publishing

Freelance Contributing Editor
Abigail Grater

Publisher
Todd Green

Art Direction + Design
CHK Design:
Christian Küsters
Barbara Nassisi

Production Editor
Elizabeth Gongde

Prepress
Artmedia, London

Printed in the United Kingdom
by Hobbs the Printers Ltd

Front cover
Coop Himmelb(l)au,
DeepHimmelblau, 2021.
© Coop Himmelb(l)au

Inside front cover
SPAN (Matias del Campo
and Sandra Manninger),
Robot Garden, Ford Motor
Company Robotics Building,
University of Michigan, Ann
Arbor, Michigan, 2020.
© SPAN

Page 1
Alisa Andrasek with Madalin
Gheorghe and Bruno Juričič,
Cloud Pergola,
Croatian National Pavilion,
Venice Architecture Biennale,
2018

ARCHITECTURAL DESIGN

May/June	Issue	Profile No.
2022	03	277

Disclaimer
The Publisher and Editors cannot be held responsible for errors or any consequences arising from the use of information contained in this journal; the views and opinions expressed do not necessarily reflect those of the Publisher and Editors, neither does the publication of advertisements constitute any endorsement by the Publisher and Editors of the products advertised.

Journal Customer Services
For ordering information, claims and any enquiry concerning your journal subscription please go to www.wileycustomerhelp .com/ask or contact your nearest office.

Americas
E: cs-journals@wiley.com
T: +1 877 762 2974

Europe, Middle East and Africa
E: cs-journals@wiley.com
T: +44 (0)1865 778 315

Asia Pacific
E: cs-journals@wiley.com
T: +65 6511 8000

Japan (for Japanese-speaking support)
E: cs-japan@wiley.com
T: +65 6511 8010

Visit our Online Customer Help available in 7 languages at www.wileycustomerhelp .com/ask

Print ISSN: 0003-8504
Online ISSN: 1554-2769

Prices are for six issues and include postage and handling charges. Individual-rate subscriptions must be paid by personal cheque or credit card. Individual-rate subscriptions may not be resold or used as library copies.

All prices are subject to change without notice.

Identification Statement
Periodicals Postage paid at Rahway, NJ 07065. Air freight and mailing in the USA by Mercury Media Processing, 1850 Elizabeth Avenue, Suite C, Rahway, NJ 07065, USA.

USA Postmaster
Please send address changes to *Architectural Design*, John Wiley & Sons Inc., c/o The Sheridan Press, PO Box 465, Hanover, PA 17331, USA.

Rights and Permissions
Requests to the Publisher should be addressed to:
Permissions Department
John Wiley & Sons Ltd
The Atrium
Southern Gate
Chichester
West Sussex PO19 8SQ
UK

F: +44 (0)1243 770 620
E: Permissions@wiley.com

Subscribe to ∆
∆ is published bimonthly and is available to purchase on both a subscription basis and as individual volumes at the following prices.

Prices
Individual copies:
£29.99 / US$45.00
Individual issues on
∆ App for iPad:
£9.99 / US$13.99
Mailing fees for print may apply

Annual Subscription Rates
Student: £97 / US$151
print only
Personal: £151 / US$236
print and iPad access
Institutional: £357 / US$666
online only
Institutional: £373 / US$695
print only
Institutional: £401 / US$748
print and online

6-issue subscription
on ∆ App for iPad:
£44.99 / US$64.99

Matias del Campo and Neil Leach are both architects and professors who have been working in the area of AI for a number of years. Both have published many articles in this field, and also teach AI in the design studio.

Matias del Campo is an Associate Professor at the Taubman College of Architecture and Urban Planning at the University of Michigan, where he is the Director of the Architecture and Artificial Intelligence Laboratory (AR²IL). He is a recipient of an Accelerate@CERN fellowship, the AIA Studio Prize and the ArtsEngine Award. He served as co-chair for the ACADIA conferences Posthuman Frontiers (2016) and Distributed Proximities (2020), as well as DigitalFUTURES 2020. He is the guest-editor of △ *Evoking Through Design* (March/April 2017), and co-author of the book *Sublime Bodies: Architectural Problems in the Postdigital Age* (Tongji University Press, 2017). With Sandra Manninger, he runs the architecture practice SPAN, known globally for its application of contemporary technologies in design. SPAN's award-winning architectural designs are informed by advanced geometry, computational methodologies and philosophical inquiry. The practice gained wide recognition for the Austrian Pavilion at the 2010 Shanghai World Expo, and more recently for the Robot Garden at the University of Michigan. SPAN's work is in the permanent collection of the FRAC Centre in Orléans, France, the Museum of Applied Arts Vienna (MAK), the Alte Pinakothek in Munich and several private collections. In 2013 the practice expanded its operations to Shanghai, where they are currently working on building projects of various scales.

Neil Leach is currently Professor at Florida International University where he directs the Doctor of Design Program. He is also Professor at Tongji University in Shanghai, and at the European Graduate School. He was previously Professor at the universities of Bath and Brighton in the UK. He has taught at many of the leading schools, including the Southern California Institute of Architecture (SCI-Arc) and University of Southern California in Los Angeles, the Architectural Association (AA) in London, Cornell and Columbia universities in New York, and the Harvard University Graduate School of Design in Cambridge, Massachusetts. He is the author of more than 40 books on architectural theory and digital design including *Machinic Processes* (China Architecture and Building Press, 2010), *Robotic Futures* (Tongji University Press, 2015), *Architectural Intelligence* (Springer, 2020) and *Architecture in the Age of AI: An Introduction to AI for Architects* (Bloomsbury, 2022). He is also the guest-editor of the △ issues *Digital Cities* (May/June 2009), *Space Architecture* (November/December 2014) and *3D Printed Body Architecture* (November/December, 2017). He is a co-founder of the educational initiative DigitalFUTURES, and has held two NASA Innovative Advanced Concepts Fellowships, where he helped to develop 3D-printing technologies for the Moon and Mars. △

Can Machines Hallucinate Architecture?

AI as Design Method

Martin Thoma,
Aurelia Aurita,
DeepDream-generated image,
2015

DeepDream image generated after 50
iterations by a neural network trained
on a dataset of images of dogs.

INTRODUCTION

MATIAS DEL CAMPO
AND NEIL LEACH

All of a sudden, AI is everywhere. It is on our phones, opening them up through facial recognition, identifying friends on Facebook and feeding us news and advertisements; on our computers, reminding us of meetings, finishing off sentences and filtering out spam; in our homes in the form of Alexa, Cortana and other AI assistants, controlling robotic floor cleaners and regulating environmental control systems; and in our cars, giving directions, finding parking spaces and notifying us if we stray out of lane. Meanwhile, self-driving cars are already here. AI is changing every aspect of our existence, and architecture is no exception, where it has already infiltrated the architectural office. Embedded in our software tools, it is changing the nature of design. The hottest topic in progressive schools and practices, AI is now the latest buzzword in architectural culture. Forget Parametricism and 3D printing – the 2020s are all about AI, the first genuinely 21st-century design technique that is revolutionising architectural culture.

This issue of Δ navigates the murky waters of this rapidly evolving field. Every week, new computer-science papers emerge that are proving valuable, interesting and informative for potential applications of AI in architecture. In computer science, AI is defined as the study and development of intelligent agents, which includes any device that perceives its environment and takes actions to maximise its chance of achieving its goals. In general, the term is applied when a machine mimics the cognitive functions associated with human beings, such as learning and problem solving. In architecture, this line of inquiry is preoccupied with two main schools of thinking. The

first is optimisation, such as possibilities for optimising floorplans, material consumption and construction site time schedules, which cover the tame problems of disciplinary considerations. At the other end of the spectrum is the inquiry into the problem of designing architecture, including creativity, intuition and sensibility, which are hard to translate into code as they elude quantification. The architecture project within this frame of consideration not only tackles the problem from an aesthetic point of view – the idea that AI can quasi-creatively generate a sensibility – but also from a series of profoundly ethical perspectives. For example, how does that posthuman frame of thinking materialise in the built environment? Do robots dream of perfect cathedrals?

What is AI?
Until now, the standard definition of AI has been that it seeks to do what human minds can do.[1] But that definition is clearly obsolete. AI can already outperform human beings in many areas. In 1997, DeepBlue beat the then world chess champion Garry Kasparov. In 2016 AlphaGo beat top player Lee Sedol at the extraordinarily complex game of Go, in which there are more potential moves than atoms in the universe. There is no longer any point in competing against AI. Indeed, in 2019 Sedol retired from the game, stating that AI 'is an entity that cannot be defeated.'[2]

In order to understand AI, we need to make a series of distinctions. The first is between AI and human intelligence. Despite what the movies portray, AI does not possess consciousness – at least for now. It might beat us at Go, but it does not even know that it is playing Go. AI has no more capacity to think or understand than our pocket calculators.

The generic term AI is hopelessly broad. Coined back in 1956, it is still used today. Yet to compare the first primitive version with the latest version – deep learning – would be like comparing a Model-T Ford with the latest Tesla. The crucial difference is that early versions of AI were programmed, whereas more recent versions of AI can learn and improve over time. These learning systems fall within the category of machine learning. Deep learning – the most advanced learning system – is a category within machine learning, itself a category within AI. Imagine them as being

Stanislas Chaillou,
ArchiGAN,
MArch thesis,
Harvard Graduate School of Design (GSD),
Cambridge, Massachusetts,
2019

By developing ArchiGAN, a Pix2Pix version of GANs, Chaillou is able to generate stacked plans for an entire building, linking furniture layout to apartment partitions to overall building footprint.

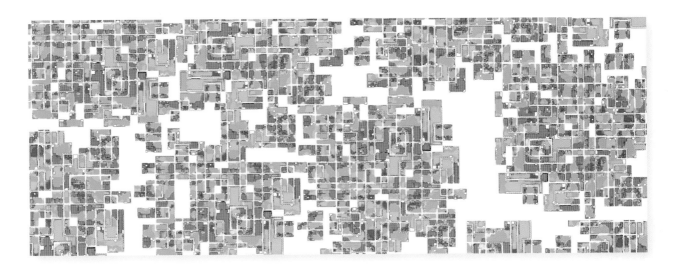

nested within each other, like Russian dolls. When anyone mentions AI these days, however, chances are that they are referring to deep learning, which gets its name from the number of layers – sometimes over 1,000 – in a neural network. A neural network is composed of 'neurons' and 'synapses' – the same terms used for the human brain – but we must therefore be careful not to equate the two. AI neurons are not the same as human neurons, just as AI learning is not the same as human learning, and artificial intelligence is not the same as human intelligence. When trying to imagine AI, forget Sophia, the humanoid robot. Think algorithms. AI is invisible. It is literally everywhere – in our phones, computers, cars and homes – but we simply cannot see it. This has two consequences. Firstly, we do not know if it is there. Secondly, we do not know if it is not there. AI can therefore be overlooked, but also exploited for marketing purposes.

How Does AI Hallucinate Images?

Image recognition, also called machine vision, is a relatively recent accomplishment within machine learning. But even more recent is the 'hallucination' of images. In 2015, Google engineer (Alexander Mordvintsev discovered that it was possible to make a neural network operate in the opposite direction. Instead of just recognising images, it could now also hallucinate images. This led to him developing the computer vision program DeepDream, which caused a major stir in artistic circles with its somewhat trippy hallucinations.[3] Train a DeepDream neural network on dogs, and it reads dogs into everything. This also opened up the possibility of style transfer, such as transferring the stripes of a zebra onto a horse, or reading an image through a neural network trained on, say, a dataset of Van Gogh paintings. In terms of image generation, however, the real breakthrough came in 2014 when computer scientist Ian Goodfellow invented generative adversarial networks (GANs).[4] These are based on two neural networks competing against each other. One, the generator, produces images, and the other, the discriminator, judges those images against a training dataset. This is a little like an art forger trying to fool an art critic into thinking that a work is genuine. The discriminator will keep rejecting output images until their quality matches the dataset images. Then, once trained, the discriminator can be removed and the generator will continue to produce convincing images.

One of the most popular forms of GAN is the StyleGAN, which *interpolates* novel variations from a dataset of several thousand images. Others, such as the CycleGAN, work with two unpaired datasets and are able to *extrapolate* images that look even more varied because they are effectively bred from two different datasets. There has been a veritable explosion in the production of GANs, such that there is now a whole zoo of different species. Another recent development has been the introduction of CLIP, a highly efficient way of generating images using Generative Pre-trained Transformer 3 (GPT-3), a natural language processing system that uses deep learning to produce human-like text and draws data from the Internet to match images

Refik Anadol,
Zaha hallucination,
2019

One of the very first images hallucinated using StyleGANs, based on a dataset of images of buildings by Zaha Hadid Architects.

Hannah Daugherty,
Mariana Moreira de Carvalho
and Imman Suleiman,
Augmented,
Imagining the Real,
Taubman College of Architecture
and Urban Planning,
University of Michigan,
Ann Arbor, Michigan,
2019

Neural networks can be trained to capture the salient features of specific architectural datasets. Here, a neural network was trained with various sets of architectural features such as gates, domes and columns. By adding a dataset of their own renderings of features the students designed, the network was trained to infuse the resulting images with their own design sensibility.

with captions. When paired with vector quantised GANS (VQGans) taming transformers for high-resolution image synthesis, CLIP can produce remarkable results based on verbal prompts.

There remain obvious challenges, however, with GANs, CLIP and other such image-generating systems. There is still no easy way of translating a 2D image into 3D form, the energy consumed in generating the images is excessive and there is little control over the system. But we can expect significant improvements in the future. Advances in computational power, better algorithms, increased competition, substantial investment, cloud computing and vastly increased data mean that AI is improving every day.

The Future of AI

AI is about predicting outcomes, and there are many predictions about its future. The next stage is when AI matches human intelligence. Shortly thereafter comes the 'singularity', as American inventor and futurist Ray Kurzweil has termed it, when the exponential development of AI will lead to an explosion of intelligence.[5] Next comes artificial general intelligence (AGI), when AI acquires consciousness. And the final stage is superintelligence, as thereafter AIs could design other AIs, and human beings would be left behind. When might these breakthroughs happen, if at all? There is no agreement on this, but as likely as not there will be no explosion. Rather, improvements will happen gradually, like a Tesla car having

SPAN (Matias del Campo and Sandra Manninger),
Latent Carceri 3,
'Experimental' series,
2020

The latent space in this example contains features learned from a large dataset of images of Giovanni Battista Piranesi's 18th-century *Le Carceri d'Invenzione*. Using a StyleGAN, it was possible to interpolate between closely clustered data points within a hidden layer, resulting in the strange versions of the *Carceri* seen here.

It is the right moment for a discussion about the impact of AI on the world of architecture

XKool Technology,
Daytime building designs,
2021

Among AI software developers for architectural practice, XKool is one of the leaders in the field in terms of generating building images using deep learning.

its software updated until it reached a certain threshold and became self-driving.

However, there is already a huge explosion of creative activity in architecture as AI captures the imagination of progressive designers. The key driver of change, though, is more likely to be commercial pressures; for example, clients are already insisting that architects use AI to guarantee their 'return of investment'.[6] In the meantime, AI will become a muse, an extension to the human imagination. With these tools, as Elon Musk notes, we become superhuman: 'You have a machine extension of yourself in the form of your phone, and your computer and all your applications. You are already superhuman.'[7]

This *D* issue documents and tracks this extraordinary explosion of AI-based creativity within the realm of architecture. Many of the contributors are experimental practitioners. They range in experience from Wolf dPrix and Coop Himmelb(l)au, one of the most established and yet progressive architectural offices in the world, exquisitely talented computational architect Alisa Andrasek, SPAN, the influential pioneers of AI methods in architecture, and Daniel Bolojan, M Casey Rehm and Immanuel Koh, three of the most technically proficient AI architects, to relatively young designers or more recent converts to AI such as Eduard Haiman, Kyle Steinfeld, Maria Kuptsova, Gabriel Esquivel, Jean Jaminet and Shane Bugni, Damjan Jovanovic and Lidija Kljakovic.

In addition, architect Wanyu He, founder of XKool Technology, discusses the application of the firm's commercial software for urban design. Others focus on performance: Theodoros Galanos and Angelos Chronis address environmental performance, Achim Menges and Thomas Wortmann describe how AI is incorporated into their fabricated designs, and Hao Zheng considers how

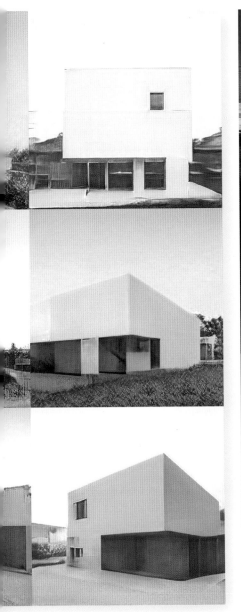

XKool Technology,
Nighttime building designs,
2021

A nighttime version of building images generated by
XKool using a version of StyleGANs.

Questions on the nature of architecture and AI are gaining enormous momentum, as the public interest in the methodology is steadily growing

Yinhang Yan,
The Walkable City,
Architecture and AI,
Tsinghua Shenzhen International
Graduate School,
Shenzhen, China,
2020

The project interrogates the ability of neural networks to infuse abstract geometric rulesets of urban design with familiar features. The resulting satellite image has sufficient familiar features to be perceived as a realistic representation of a city. At the same time there are aspects of defamiliarisation and estrangement at play that draw the observer's attention to the uncanny qualities of the depiction.

AI can model dragonfly wings and other structures. More theoretical contributions include that from Behnaz Farahi, who uses AI in a feminist critique of the male gaze.

Media artist Refik Anadol, who uses buildings as both his material and his 'canvas', AI artists Sophia Crespo and Feileacan McCormick, new media theorist Lev Manovich and neuroscientist Alexandra Carlson all also offer important messages for architects.

Learning Machines and Human Ingenuity

Posing questions about authorship, ingenuity, imagination and creativity, this *D* issue interrogates the role of humans in an AI-assisted design universe. All of a sudden, architecture projects emerge from vast amounts of data, crushed through graphics processing units (GPUs) running sophisticated deep-learning algorithms able to surpass the ability of humans to compute data in unprecedented numbers. At the other end of the design agency spectrum is the human capacity to extrapolate possible new design methods from the results presented by neural networks, the ability to find inspiration in mistakes, and the nuanced sensibility to infuse space with additional meaning than the raw materiality would suggest. Questions on the nature of architecture and AI are gaining enormous momentum, as

the public interest in the methodology is steadily growing. It is the right moment for a discussion about the impact of AI on the world of architecture. Some of the most surprising aspects emerge when the techniques presented in this *D* learn from inherently different architectural data, such as using different historical datasets of architecture in combination with contemporary architecture, resulting in weird mashups that challenge disciplinary positions and provoke novel disciplinary trajectories – familiar yet different, comprehensive yet exotic, alien yet beautiful. *D*

Notes
1. Margaret Boden, *AI: Its Nature and Future*, Oxford University Press (Oxford), 2016, p 1.
2. 'Go Master Lee Says He Quits Unable to Win Over AI Go Players', Yonhap News Agency, 27 November 2019: https://en.yna.co.kr/view/AEN20191127004800315.
3. https://deepdreamgenerator.com/.
4. Martin Giles, 'The GANfather: The Man Who's Given Machines the Gift of Imagination', *MIT Technology Review*, 21 February 2018: www.technologyreview.com/s/610253/the-ganfather-the-man-whos-given-machines-the-gift-of-imagination/.
5. Ray Kurzweil, *The Singularity is Near*, Viking (New York), 2005. See also Peter Rejcek, 'Can Futurists Predict the Year of the Singularity?', SingularityHub, 31 March 2017: https://singularityhub.com/2017/03/31/can-futurists-predict-the-year-of-the-singularity/#sm.00001ep69rsevnd56vi0hrvmkpsor.
6. Neil Leach, *Architecture in the Age of Artificial Intelligence: An Introduction to AI for Architects*, Bloomsbury (London), 2022, p 121.
7. 'Elon Musk's Message on Artificial Superintelligence – ASI', *Science Time*, 24 October 2020: www.youtube.com/watch?v=ZCeOsdcQObI&feature=youtu.be.

Yara Feghali / FollyFeastLab,
3rd Street,
2020

Façades of buildings on 3rd Street, Los Angeles, transformed by a convolutional neural network (CNN) trained on Bavarian Rococo art and architecture, by Lebanese architect Yara Feghali of experimental design studio FollyFeastLab.

Wolf dPrix, Karolin Schmidbaur,
Daniel Bolojan and Efilena Baseta

THE LEGACY SKETCH MACHINE

FROM ARTIFICIAL TO ARCHITECTURAL INTELLIGENCE

Coop Himmelb(l)au,
DeepHimmelblau
research project,
2021

Latent space algorithmic explorations. Once a sample (left image) has been chosen from the network's latent space, the designers can search for samples that are similar or dissimilar in their features (smaller images to the right). The latent space of the DeepHimmelblau network can be explored using an algorithmic approach that allows for a strategic search using a number of techniques designed to enable intuitive navigation.

In the office of Coop Himme(l)blau in Vienna, a series of software machine-learning protocols and practices continually reinterpret the firm's past and future projects, unleashing new work and possibilities for architectures yet to exist. Here **Wolf dPrix, Karolin Schmidbaur, Daniel Bolojan and Efilena Baseta** explain the uses and some of the outputs of this suite of tools.

Looking back over years of DeepHimmelblau research offers an excellent opportunity to stand back and take stock. When Coop Himmelb(l)au (CHBL) first started experimenting with AI, investigations centred around how individual processes within the practice's workflow could be fed into the machine so that the practice could be enriched by the unique new perspectives offered by the output. Over time, these neural networks have evolved into a novel, interconnected palette of networks and tools, resulting in a new reading of the research. It is a reading that operates at a meta level and repositions the research as a tool to offer new insights into the legacy of the practice.

Coop Himmelb(l)au,
DeepHimmelblau research project,
2021

DeepHimmelblau sample output based on geomorphological samples and CHBL project samples. Each node network learns the semantic representation and the underlying compositional rules of the architectural and non-architectural domains in order to perform coherent network-to-network cross-resolution blends and cross-layer feature combinations.

Coop Himmelb(l)au Universe

CHBL has over 50 years' experience of extensive architectural production that is manifested, archived and available in thousands of project representations in analogue and digital formats such as hand sketches, physical models, visualisations, photographs, 2D drawings, 3D drawings and models, details and built manifestations. This oeuvre offers a perfect database for the application of neural networks and other machine-learning tools. The multimodal representations are an ideal vehicle for training the DeepHimmelblau network, as neural networks require vast amounts of data.

As the name 'DeepHimmelblau' suggests, the project is an investigation into the work of the practice utilising deep-learning tools. Drawing inspiration from knowledge in the field of AI, it is staking out new ground through the development of its own novel neural networks for applications in architectural practice. In this context, DeepHimmelblau explores the possibility – in connection with human beings – of teaching machines to be creative, to interpret, perceive, propose new designs, augment design processes and augment design creativity.

What are the possibilities that open up if a practice, in addition to its ongoing work, can now (a) uncover new insights from the archives of its entire recorded project history and combine them with the added intelligence of

in-house developed novel neural networks, and (b) connect these new insights with its ongoing work – instead of simply continuing to evolve, in the traditional way, from the experiences, knowledge and creativity of certain individuals who rely on the fact that experiences are communicated amongst them, generation after generation?

While there is some advantage in developing and disseminating insights into the tradition of the practice, there is also a risk with having some of these processes automated or augmented and delegated to a machine. In particular, does this research depart from the work's tradition of human inspiration, intuition, spontaneity, directness and emotionality?

The Open Process

The open process is a working method that is open-ended and non-determinate. It is a complex form of open dialogue, in which different people, tools, intuitive, interpretative and analytical steps can be combined, referenced and negotiated. The open process is different from a closed, linear process, in which the input parameters directly influence the outcome of the process in a simple cause-and-effect way.

When CHBL was established in 1968, it set out to revolutionise architecture. The idea of the complex operations of the open process were initiated by the sketch, which in itself is both rich in meaning and open for interpretation. The manifestation of an idea for a project through the sketch starts a dialogue, in which the sketch is experienced, communicated and step by step translated into architecture. It is the sketch that starts a process, but only through the process itself will the sketch be translated into a building.

Here is the Coop Himmelb(l)au approach to the design process: 'Without knowing where this will lead us, we begin to condense and shorten the time of the design process, i.e. we talk about the project for a long time, but without ever thinking of the spatial consequences. And then, all of a sudden, there's the drawing on the paper, on the table, and, at the same time, we start on the working model. Coop Himmelb(l)au is a team. When we draw, the architecture is put into words, the sketch narrated to the partner, the project presented for being experienced, the experienced moment of design communicated.'[1]

With the advent of digital tools in the early 1990s, the former predominantly analogue design process, based on the sketch, evolved into an intricate design workflow in which novel digital technologies could be utilised as needed and appropriate. Photogrammetry, digitisation and scanning began to replace the analogue techniques of measuring physical models; parametric models have made complex geometry describable and controllable; the robotic arm expands the field of possibilities for design, fabrication, materialisation and construction; and digital simulations and animations add the dimension of time in planning, representation and theoretical models.

True to the idea of the open process, however, which relies on incongruencies, translations and disconnections

as a motor for new solutions to emerge, the entire process could never be replaced by a single, discrete, automated computational process – as may be possible in a more linear way of working. Rather, in the CHBL nonlinear workflow, computational tools are not seen as a replacement, but as a way of enriching and enhancing the design process while also optimising, economising and partially automating parts of it.

So, what are the implications of incorporating the DeepHimmelblau network into the practice's open design process?

Augmentation Versus Automation

Interestingly, the Russian chess master Garry Kasparov came to a similar conclusion about the value of process, when experimenting with human–machine interactions in chess and trying to determine which modes of interaction could be more efficient in improving a player's competitive advantage.

Kasparov discovered that having a well-defined process is likely to be a better strategy than simply having a combination of best player and best machine. He observed that 'a weak human player plus a machine plus a better process is superior to a very powerful machine alone, but more remarkably, is superior to a strong human player plus machine and an inferior process'. In his words: 'Our aim should be that of ... intelligence amplification, to use information technology as a tool to enhance human decisions instead of replacing them with autonomous AI Systems'.[2]

Geometry-based latent space snapshot. The novel 3D DeepHimmelblau network node recognises projects in three dimensions and allows for formal interpolations. Not only is the network capable of generating exceptionally high-quality 3D design samples, but it also gives users control over the produced samples at different design stages by adjusting the style of latent vectors and noise.

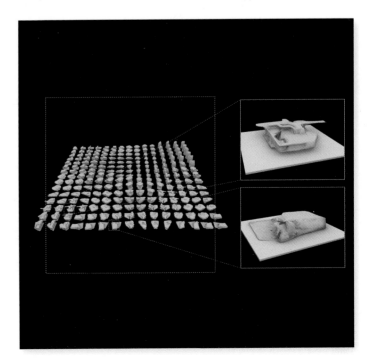

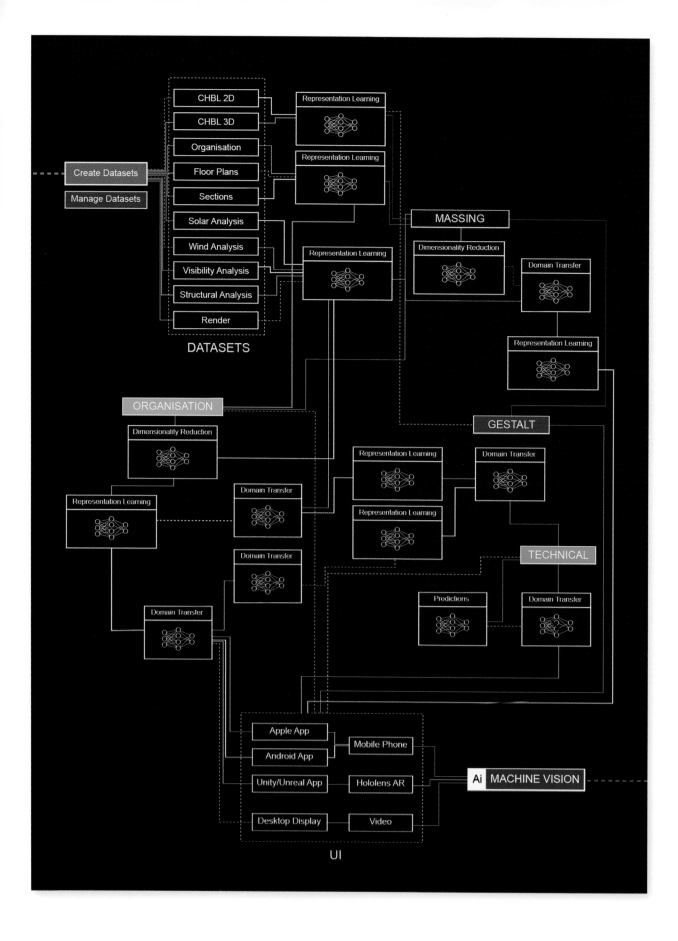

Aligning these observations with the practice's open process workflow, the initial and immediate strategy of DeepHimmelblau is obvious and consequential: while some of DeepHimmelblau's network nodes may automate partial processes and thus streamline the overall workflow, the main potential lies in finding ways to amplify the intelligence of the practice, summed up in the term 'augmentation' versus 'automation'. This is achieved by combining machine with human intelligence in techniques of reciprocal interaction that augment and further inspire the work.

What human–machine interaction techniques can we introduce to further inspire creativity? What modes of human–machine feedback loops can be constructed, where new workflows and technologies can be created and thereafter inspire and influence us?

Interconnected AI Processes

The novel DeepHimmelblau network draws inspiration from various networks such as variational autoencoders, diffusion models, context encoders, Pix2Pix for image translation, CycleGAN for domain translation, StyleGAN image synthesis processes, DeepLab for semantic segmentation, and many other machine-learning techniques. The network has different nodes for discrete design tasks such as image-to-image translation, 2D and 3D domain transfers, representation learning and synthesis. Additional nodes that understand project semantics and organisational strategies from a 3D perspective are currently being developed, where aspects of form and content are explored in parallel, with the goal of ultimately being able to link them into three-dimensional structures that have meaning as architecture.

As CHBL's semantics and style are not homogeneous, one of the main challenges was how to design the DeepHimmelblau network so that it learns the correct semantic representation of the projects without biasing the network towards a more prevalent style represented by a particular project. How can we design the network in such a way that it weighs the project's semantics correctly?

In the absence of labelled target examples, our network's feature maps and feature extractors are designed to learn how to semantically align distributions, thereby improving the network's ability to understand the underlying semantics represented in the input dataset. Furthermore, the multimodal (images, segmentation maps, depth maps, text, 3D) training ability of the node-based network contributes significantly to improvements in learning the correct semantic representation.

The node-based structure of the DeepHimmelblau network enables task-dependent strategies of interconnected nodes to be established in response to discrete design tasks, specific design problems or the nature of any given investigation. The different nodes are categorised following specific architectural criteria such as technical, organisational or formal issues, while still utilising the potential resource of the entire multimodal CHBL archive.

The network not only allows the connection of multiple nodes, but also permits the semantic levels of the various

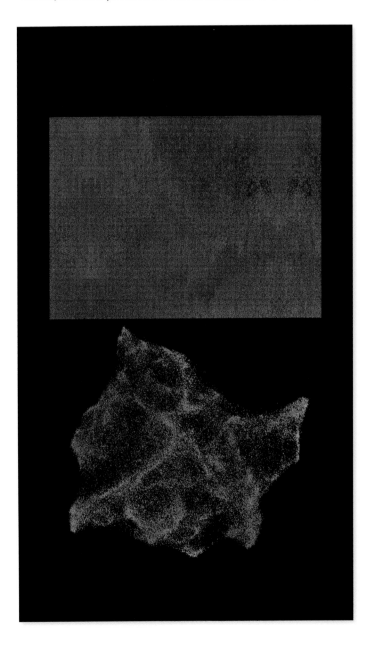

Coop Himmelb(l)au,
DeepHimmelblau research project,
2021

opposite: Diagram of the DeepHimmelblau network's workflow illustrating the development of task-dependent interconnected nodes. DeepHimmelblau is integrated into the existing open process workflow due to the network's node-based structure.

right: Snapshot of the latent space of the DeepHimmelblau network, a universe of design possibilities. Through a web-based interface, the method enables designers to engage with the DeepHimmelblau network in a very intuitive manner.

Image-based latent space snapshot. The semantics used to build the DeepHimmelblau universe (middle) define the methods by which the database can be accessed in an open feedback process. The DeepHimmelblau network's latent space can be explored by projecting any given design sample (left) into the network's memory and querying for examples with comparable compositional characteristics (right).

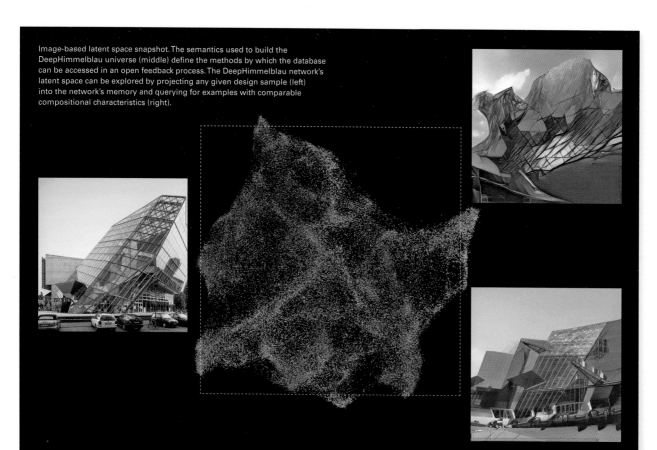

Latent space query. With the goal of lowering the DeepHimmelblau network's access threshold for the practice's designers, the network supports text-based searches alongside image, plan-based and 3D-based ones. The latent space query technique examines an input text or design description, determines its semantics, and searches the DeepHimmelblau Generator Network for images that express those semantics.

Query	1	2	3	4	5	6	7	8	9	10	11	12	13	14	15	16
A panelised façade	0.245	0.248	0.240	0.242	0.236	0.251	0.239	0.220	0.221	0.242	0.294	0.252	0.247	0.230	0.328	0.280
An irregular-shaped office tower	0.261	0.288	0.261	0.225	0.203	0.254	0.226	0.255	0.239	0.265	0.230	0.299	0.275	0.212	0.273	0.231
An open public space with an overhanging roof	0.255	0.250	0.261	0.265	0.247	0.261	0.219	0.243	0.226	0.249	0.255	0.238	0.261	0.248	0.247	0.255
A building with two intersecting volumes	0.276	0.280	0.284	0.243	0.247	0.260	0.232	0.249	0.247	0.265	0.251	0.277	0.263	0.260	0.274	0.260
A building with a double cone shape and triangular panelisation	0.266	0.255	0.269	0.230	0.215	0.270	0.218	0.225	0.250	0.253	0.221	0.261	0.258	0.233	0.259	0.235
A convention centre, with a plinth and cantilevering roof	0.256	0.248	0.258	0.276	0.262	0.254	0.258	0.242	0.222	0.243	0.266	0.255	0.247	0.248	0.246	0.267
Concept for a convention centre and hotel complex	0.297	0.277	0.284	0.253	0.256	0.282	0.248	0.257	0.266	0.305	0.274	0.273	0.277	0.291	0.293	0.283
Concept of an office building with two towers	0.267	0.272	0.269	0.250	0.226	0.255	0.235	0.239	0.241	0.261	0.239	0.285	0.269	0.252	0.290	0.266
Open cinema centre with a floating roof and open gardens	0.280	0.250	0.265	0.270	0.257	0.243	0.222	0.237	0.235	0.263	0.272	0.238	0.240	0.290	0.246	0.282
Open cinema centre with a floating roof	0.270	0.240	0.254	0.270	0.264	0.247	0.232	0.239	0.229	0.259	0.280	0.231	0.244	0.289	0.243	0.270
A tower with glass façade	0.253	0.287	0.250	0.284	0.215	0.246	0.251	0.250	0.241	0.259	0.234	0.295	0.274	0.223	0.268	0.237
A building with glass façade, a plinth, overhanging volume and façade perforations	0.298	0.285	0.284	0.274	0.269	0.275	0.279	0.277	0.265	0.284	0.266	0.296	0.300	0.280	0.270	0.282
Office building with triangular panellisation	0.223	0.214	0.235	0.252	0.203	0.226	0.231	0.279	0.213	0.235	0.258	0.242	0.243	0.294	0.225	0.270

node network layers to be combined, blended and swapped between network nodes. This enables the creation of feedback loops across design scales, and the creation of dynamic feedback loops of interaction between machine and designer within a nonlinear open process framework. As a result, degrees of agency are enabled at multiple levels of design, allowing design intentionality to be encoded at various discrete levels.

Additional network nodes enable classification, sorting, filtering, strategic search and the exploration of the various latent spaces addressing different levels of design to be carried out, through various intuitive, algorithmic, image-based and text-based modalities. These nodes aim to lower the access threshold to the various networks for non-specialists (architects in the office) by providing intuitive control of the latent spaces, learned features, node network parameters and network blending strategies via a user-friendly interface.

Unique to this interconnected process is the goal and ability of the network to stage possibilities for feedback and translation that allow reciprocal interactions between the analogue and digital worlds, and between ideas or needs of new design problems and the combined knowledge of the database. The most promising and challenging terrain in the explorations currently is twofold: the questions of (1) what possibilities for design are latent in the vast Coop Himmelb(l)au universe that has so far been generated, and (2) how to make this latent space even more accessible for the architects in the office. In other words, how do we best specify the semantics built into this universe so we can find the best ways to search its potential and have it deliver meaningful outputs?

A Novel AI Universe

As we take stock, we now look at a fruitful and intricate DeepHimmelblau network containing a vast spectrum of different nodes with the possibility of reconnecting those with and within the open design process. By drawing information from the entire CHBL archive, we have created a novel Coop Himmelblau Universe, and thus have the potential to add a new dimension into the work, which is now available to be tapped into.

With this in mind, the call is once again on us, the human beings who comprise Coop Himmelb(l)au to form a dialogue with the machine, to discover ways and methods to read and interpret this new machine inspiration and translate it back into CHBL's work. Does this digital experiment bring the work a step away from its tradition of human inspiration, from spontaneity, directness, the emotional and inspired? No, we are back to reading the sketch again, the legacy's sketch, beautifully loaded up with a new deep meaning. ∆

Notes
1. Gerald Zugmann, *Blue Universe: Transforming Models into Pictures – Architectural Projects by Coop Himmelb(l)au*, Hatje Cantz (Ostfildern-Ruit), 2002, p 83.
2. Garry Kasparov, *Deep Thinking: Where Machine Intelligence Ends and Human Creativity Begins*, PublicAffairs (New York), 2017, p 214.

The legacy's sketch offers inspiration and new machine insights that potentially bear solutions for future problems. Similarly to how feathers were developed by nature without dinosaurs ever thinking about flying, AI is a tool that will one day allow architects to fly.

Daniel Bolojan

CREATIVE AI

Assistant Professor at Florida Atlantic University School of Architecture, founder of Nonstandardstudio and a PhD student in Vienna, **Daniel Bolojan** researches AI-augmented systems that have the potential to liberate architects' and designers' creativity. This is not to say that human imagination and machine learning should be equated; they are very different in the way they function and respond to the world, but when combined they offer new creative opportunities.

AUGMENTING DESIGN POTENCY

Daniel Bolojan / Nonstandardstudio,
Machine Perceptions:
Gaudí + Neural Networks,
2021

The system, which features six interconnected networks, allows for design intention to be encoded at various design levels. Methods such as cross-network feature blending enable the designer to emphasise or de-emphasise desired semantic features.

23

Despite being in its early stages, the application of AI in architecture is already yielding promising results that will undoubtedly reshape the architectural field. Every week, new examples of machines that can paint, write poems, design everyday objects, compose songs or write movie scripts are introduced as a result of rapid advances in the field of AI. These technological advances call into question our design methodologies, understanding of our culture, and interactions with the world around us, among other things. Two factors that have helped to cause such a significant disruption are the sheer volume of data generated every day, as well as the speed at which computers can process data and extract insights. In this context, a more general discussion about AI and creativity has begun to emerge. Is it possible for machines to be creative? Is it possible for machines to be intelligent?

Often, AI outcomes are regarded as creative because they entail a degree of novelty and an appreciation for novelty, which is critical since if something is too novel for us to appreciate, it has no value to us. Current AI models, such as deep neural networks (DNNs), see and perceive the world in a fundamentally different way to how humans do,[1] even though they are inspired by the way our brain works. Given that we have no means of knowing if another entity is intelligent or creative in the same way as we are, and know very little about our own creative methodology, Alan Turing, the founder of modern computer science, believed that the only way to evaluate that entity's intelligence is via its behaviour.[2] Is machine creativity the same as human creativity, or is it a different kind of creativity? Is our goal to create machines that mimic human intelligence and creativity, or are we aiming to create machines that are capable of being intelligent and creative in their own right?

FROM EXPERT SYSTEMS TO LEARNING SYSTEMS

AI is a relatively new field. In computer science, there are two main approaches to developing intelligent systems: expert systems and learning systems. Expert systems were very popular in the 1970s–80s, whereas learning systems gained popularity around 2006. The transition from expert systems to learning systems is one of the most significant shifts we are witnessing today in computer science and architecture. Expert systems are knowledge systems composed of two subsystems: a knowledge base, which specifies rules, and an inference engine, which applies the rules to known facts to derive new facts. Learning systems, on the other hand, are systems based on neural networks, that derive solutions from raw data. Expert systems require inputs and rules to derive results; supervised learning systems require inputs and results to derive rules; and unsupervised learning systems require inputs to derive the underlying rules. Expert systems need a human 'expert' to input information into the knowledge base, while learning systems do not require such an 'expert'. Rather than relying on hardcoded solutions, learning systems learn solutions from first principles. Neural networks, which are inspired by the structure and function of the human brain as well as the way humans acquire certain types of knowledge, are examples of learning systems. They do not learn through hardcoded solutions, but rather by example.

Expert systems, such as rule-based parametric design, and computer-aided design systems are widely used in

Daniel Bolojan / Nonstandardstudio, Machine Perceptions: Gaudí + Neural Networks, 2021

The extrapolative capability of the system enables the generation of novel compositions that retain the semantics of the underlying architectural domain.

The Network Feature map represents the output of one filter applied to the previous layer. The provided filter is drawn one pixel at a time across the previous layer. The activation of the neuron occurs at each location, and the output is collected in the feature map.

architecture, and feature functions and methods with hardcoded knowledge. To generate meaningful results, parametric models must be constructed at an appropriate level of abstraction and with the geometrical constraint interdependencies properly established. In a parametric model, all potential outcomes are given *a priori* in the starting condition. As a result, design has been reduced to a selection process rather than a creative generative one.

What are the implications of the advent of learning systems in architectural design? Can machines learn architecturally relevant semantic information without relying on hardcoded information, as is the case of parametric models? In this context, the ongoing research project Machine Perceptions: Gaudí + Neural Networks aims to develop neural networks capable of identifying relevant geometrical principles, structural and compositional features in non-architectural domains and samples representing the Sagrada Família (1882–present), the Roman Catholic basilica in Barcelona designed by Spanish architect Antoni Gaudí.

MACHINE PERCEPTION
While people may identify and untangle different semantic aspects of what they see subconsciously, neural networks can exhibit similar behaviour after learning from a large enough collection of samples. They learn automatically to disentangle semantic features in a dataset, allowing particular features to be isolated and controlled at any given level.

Neither our conscious visual representations of reality nor our perceptions of reality correspond to a direct mapping of the physical world in which we live. We make sense of the world by recreating and interpreting our previous experiences. Our previous experiences act as a filter for how we understand, comprehend and perceive the world around us in the present and in the future, respectively.[3] Our architectural education shapes how we see, understand and draw inspiration from the world, as well as how we think about it. Similarly the learning process and results of neural networks are very often constrained by the features map, datasets, and biases presented in the dataset.

MACHINE CREATIVITY
While AI may exhibit some form of limited intelligence and creativity, and similarities between machines and humans can be drawn in terms of both qualities, the two should not be equated. If we are to believe the world-renowned cognitive scientist Margaret Boden, human creativity could be classified as combinatorial, exploratory and transformational,[4] whereas, according to Demis Hassabis – CEO and co-founder of DeepMind – machine creativity can be classified as interpolative, extrapolative and invention.[5] Interpolative creativity entails averaging samples from the entire field of possibilities, and the resulting average can be thought of as something novel contained within the domain of the input training dataset. Extrapolative creativity on the other hand entails a higher level of machine creativity that is not based on simple dataset averaging, with the network capable of generating genuinely new samples outside the domain of the input dataset. While neural networks are quite capable of interpolative creativity – they excel at

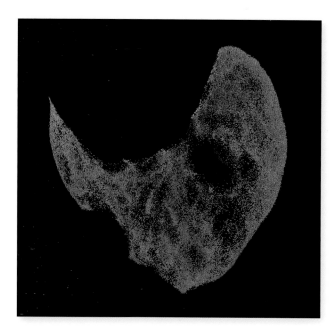

Daniel Bolojan / Nonstandardstudio,
Machine Perceptions:
Gaudí + Neural Networks,
2021

above: Visualisation of network 4 latent space. Using classification and dimensionality reduction methods, a placement rule is established in which samples with similar features are placed closer together and those with dissimilar features are placed farther apart.

below: Once network 5 has learned the representation of the Sagrada Família domain, it can generate additional synthetic samples that mimic Sagrada Família via interpolation. Extrapolation capability is demonstrated by the system through the use of interconnected processes operating at various semantic levels.

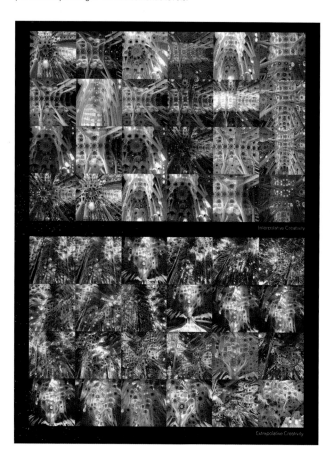

averaging samples and recognising patterns in data – only a few are capable of extrapolative creativity, and none are capable of invention.

As designers, we often engage in an 'interpolative' or combinatorial mode of creativity, in which we create/construct interpolations of previously known concepts/ideas. Currently, parametric design is one of the most common modes of computational design in architecture, in which computation is reduced to a hierarchical structure of associative constraints, allowing for a flexible tool of exploration.[6] Creating design variations or design procedures using parametric models is a common architectural practice today. As with interpolative machine creativity, a parametric model's results may be considered innovative due to their well-known structure; they also may appear novel due to unusual values of the defining variables;[7] however, the results remain constrained by the parametric model's *a priori* defined parameter space.[8] Parametric models and expert systems in general are not able to extrapolate as no new variation is generated outside the predefined parameter space.

Can we use learning systems to help us expand our constrained design spaces? After all, even though design may be thought of as a constantly expanding and contracting space of possibilities, our own past experiences and training as architects limits the way we evaluate design outputs. Since we have no means of knowing whether we currently operate within a global maximum or local minima in design terms, what we perceive to be a good output is often a fairly conventional design.

AGENCY OF DESIGN

The Sagrada Família exhibits meaningful tectonics that are defined by the building's underlying composition and are confined to a conventional nave, symmetry and seriality. The objective of the Machine Perceptions: Gaudí + Neural Networks research project is to use deep-learning techniques and develop strategies to liberate the tectonic detail by releasing its complexity, novelty and structural features. The strategies developed enable the intricate tectonic details and structural properties to be played out on more complex compositions (for example, by freeing up the plan, which is required in the contemporary world), provide access at various compositional scales, and thus increase the composition's design potency. The goal of this research is not to conserve or replicate the Sagrada Família, or to create mere interpolations of the learned representation, but to gain insights into and develop geometrical strategies for liberating the composition while retaining the underlying composition of tectonic details, resulting in new novel compositions. While human curation of the dataset is important, it provides a limited level of agency. Similar to parametric design, where design possibilities are specified in the starting condition, relying solely on datasets to encode design intent and intelligence leads to highly restrictive solutions. Thus, it is crucial that strategies, mechanisms and methodologies are developed that allow for design intention and intelligence to be

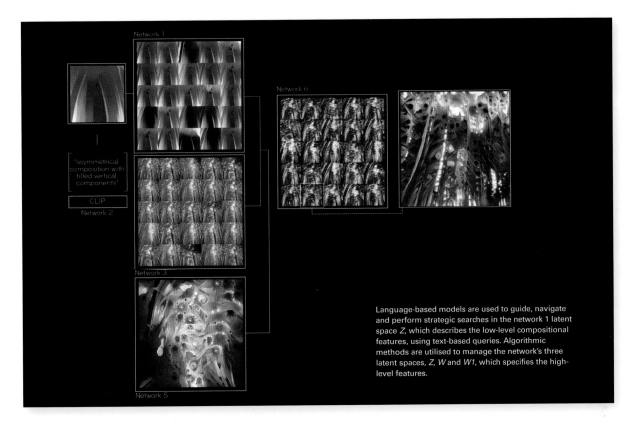

Language-based models are used to guide, navigate and perform strategic searches in the network 1 latent space *Z*, which describes the low-level compositional features, using text-based queries. Algorithmic methods are utilised to manage the network's three latent spaces, *Z*, *W* and *W1*, which specifies the high-level features.

encoded at multiple levels of design. Previously mentioned classification of machine creativity types – interpolative, extrapolative and invention – should be viewed as a degree, a spectrum, rather than a discrete classification.

Multiple task-specific systems capable of interpolative or extrapolative machine creativity are linked together in this research, as extrapolative creativity requires interpolative creativity. Similar to AlphaGo,[9] which has three interacting networks – a policy network, value network and tree search – the system developed in this research has six interconnected networks, each of which addresses discrete design tasks at various levels. Interpolative abilities are featured by networks 1, 2, 3 and 5, while limited extrapolative abilities are featured by networks 4 and 6. Network 1 is learning the representation[10] of lower-level composition features, while network 2 performs text-based queries[11] to enable a more strategic search of the lower-level latent space and provide a mechanism for encoding design intentions. Network 3 is learning the representation of the non-architectural domain, from which high-level features will be transferred, while network 5 is learning the representations of the architectural domain – in this case, the Sagrada Família. The latent space of the two networks 3 and 5 serves as the input dataset for network 6, which is responsible for transfers across the domains represented by networks 3 and 5. Because network 4 is generated by retaining the low-level structure of network 1 and blending it with the high-level features of network 3, its output samples inherit low- and high-level features from both networks 1 and 3.

The approach enables the creation of novel compositions that are not limited by conventional compositional constraints while preserving the connections in tectonic details. The resulting interconnected system allows for design intentions to be encoded at different levels in the system through multimodal algorithmic, text-based, image-based and gradient-based inputs. While the system shows extrapolative capabilities on its own, the shared agency between the human designer and the machine may benefit both: human designer and machine. ◢

NOTES
1. See Adam R Kosiorek *et al*, 'Stacked Capsule Autoencoders', in Hanna M Wallach *et al* (eds), *Advances in Neural Information Processing Systems 32: NeurIPS 2019*, Curran Associates (Vancouver), 2019, pp 15486–96.
2. Alan M Turing, 'Computing Machinery and Intelligence', *Mind* 59, 1950, pp 433–60.
3. See Jacques Derrida, *The Truth in Painting*, University of Chicago Press (Chicago, IL), 1987.
4. Margaret Boden, 'Creativity and Artificial Intelligence', *Artificial Intelligence* 103, 1997, pp 347–56.
5. Demis Hassabis, lecture at the Rothschild Foundation, Waddesdon, Buckinghamshire, 10 October 2018: www.youtube.com/watch?v=d-bvsJWmqlc&t=1945s.
6. See Robert Woodbury, *Elements of Parametric Design*, Routledge (London), 2010.
7. See John Gero, 'Design Prototypes: A Knowledge Representation Schema for Design', *AI Magazine* 11 (4), 1990, pp 26–36.
8. See Woodbury, *op cit*.
9. See David Silver *et al*, 'Mastering the Game of Go with Deep Neural Networks and Tree Search', *Nature* 529, 2016, pp 484–9.
10. See Yoshua Bengio, Aaron C Courville and Pascal Vincent, 'Representation Learning: A Review and New Perspectives', *IEEE Transactions on Pattern Analysis and Machine Intelligence* 35, 2013, pp 1798–828.
11. See Alec Radford *et al*, 'Learning Transferable Visual Models From Natural Language Supervision', in Marina Meila and Tong Zhang (eds), *Proceedings of the 38th International Conference on Machine Learning (ICML)*, 2021, pp 8748–63.

Refik Anadol

Refik Anadol Studio,
Infinity Room,
Istanbul,
2015

Infinity Room suggests a particular aesthetic of infinity by combining the boundlessness of space with the endless permutations of machine intelligence.

SPACE
MIND
MACH

IN THE
OF A
NE

IMMERSIVE
NARRATIVES

Director and founder of Refik Anadol Studio in Los Angeles and researcher in the Department of Design Media Arts at the University of California, Los Angeles (UCLA), **Refik Anadol** collaborates with machine intelligence to create multi-sensory immersive environments that reinvigorate the public realm, animate surroundings and explore the non-linearity of time. His works are colourful, thoughtful, experimental and engaging.

If machines can 'learn' or 'process' individual and collective memories, can they also dream about them? Does being an AI in the 21st century simply mean not forgetting anything? What does it mean to be human in the age of artificial intelligence when time-spaces can be expanded and transformed into *multiverse* experiences in the mind of a machine? When I walked into Google's Artists & Machine Intelligence Program in 2016 to start my residency on a research project at the intersection of neuroscience and architecture, these were the primary questions that later became the building blocks of my 'Machine Hallucinations' series – an ongoing exploration of data aesthetics based on collective visual memories of space, nature and urban environments. In my mind, 'the future of being human' confronted the complex question of quantifying consciousness through AI-based digital aesthetics. My goal was to collaborate with the machine-mind to redefine consciousness with a new vocabulary of world-making. With the establishment of Refik Anadol Studio (RAS), we began exploring how the perception of time and space were radically changing now that machines dominated our everyday lives and how the digital age and AI allowed for new aesthetic techniques to create enriched immersive environments.

Refik Anadol Studio,
Archive Dreaming,
SALT Galata, Istanbul,
2017

opposite: By training a neural network
with images of 1,700,000 documents
at the SALT research centre in
Istanbul, Refik Anadol Studio created
an immersive installation to reframe
the memories, histories and cultures
of the city.

Refik Anadol Studio,
Pladis: Data Universe,
Istanbul,
2018

below: In this project, RAS explored
the concept of infinity by transgressing
the boundaries of a traditional viewing
experience and transforming the
conventional flat cinema projection
screen into a three-dimensional
kinetic and architectonic space.

Since 2016, RAS has been conducting interdisciplinary
research on the relation between the human mind,
architecture, aesthetics and new media forms to speculate
computational and representational concerns about
the perception of environment(s). These inquiries have
centred around a pioneering concept that emerged from
our art practice to become a research unit: Latent Cinema.
Thinking and producing at the intersection of AI, aesthetics
and architecture, the studio has been reflecting on new
forms of narrating collective memory and history by
creating immersive spaces and interactive artworks that
would transform traditional understandings of the public
sphere. Experiments with synaesthesia, networked media
and interconnectivity through interactive, site-specific
installations are used to represent machine-based, latent
data universes in urban locations that enable deliberation
on what media art scholars Janine Marchessault and Susan
Lord call 'cinema's expanding architectures'.[1]

Machine Hallucinations

Simulating non-linearity of time and experiences in immersive environments comes with the interdisciplinary question of how new media art and post-digital architecture can help artists speculate new definitions of consciousness and intelligence. From this perspective, cognitive neuroscientist Anil Seth's research on consciousness and hallucination poses inspirational challenges to define the scope of such immersive art projects. Seth proposes that normal perception can be seen as a kind of 'controlled hallucination', and that the brain uses predictions and models 'to best anticipate the flow of noisy and ambiguous sensory signals in which it is continually immersed'.[2] What the 'Machine Hallucinations' series seeks to uncover is the possibility of creating a similar immersion experience through art to feel like we are in the mind of a machine-brain that hallucinates based on the data that it artificially 'perceives'.

Since the inception of 'Machine Hallucinations' in 2016, I have been utilising machine intelligence as a collaborator with human consciousness, specifically deep convolutional generative adversarial network (DCGAN), personalised general adversarial network (PGAN) and StyleGAN algorithms trained on vast datasets to unfold unrecognised layers of external realities. Collections of data from digital archives and publicly available resources are processed with machine-learning classification models to filter out people, noise and irrelevant data points. The sorted image datasets are then clustered into thematic categories to better understand the semantic context of the data universe. This expanding data universe not only represents the interpolation of data as synthesis, but also becomes a latent cosmos in which hallucinative potential is the main currency of artistic creativity.

As a masterfully curated multi-channel experience, 'Machine Hallucinations' brings a self-regenerating element of surprise to the audience and offers a new form of sensational autonomy via cybernetic serendipity. For ARTECHOUSE's New York City location, a special edition was created in the form of a data universe in 1,025 latent dimensions by deploying machine-learning algorithms on over 100 million photographic memories of New York City found in social networks. *Machine Hallucination: NYC* thus generated a novel form of synaesthetic storytelling through its multilayered manipulation of a vast visual archive beyond the conventional limits of the camera and existing cinematographic techniques. The resulting artwork was a 30-minute experimental cinema, presented in 16K resolution, that visualised the story of New York through the city's collective memories which constituted its deeply hidden consciousness.

Refik Anadol Studio,
Machine Hallucination: NYC,
ARTECHOUSE, New York City,
2019

Machine Hallucination: NYC is a 30-minute experimental cinema, presented in 16K resolution, that visualises a data-based narrative of New York City by deploying machine-learning algorithms on over 100 million photographic memories of the city found publicly in social networks.

Cities and urban architectures served as rich sources of narrative inspiration as countless iconic urban locations were treated as if they were living organisms with multiple layers of history and sensation projected on them

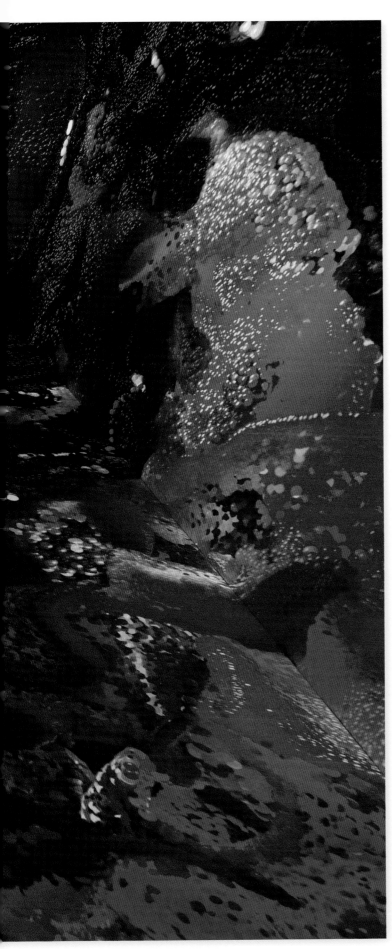

Refik Anadol Studio,
'Machine Memoirs: Space',
Istanbul,
2021

'Machine Memoirs: Space' was a free public art exhibition that brought together the studio's richly diverse works on the theme of space exploration, inspired by a recent collaboration with the NASA Jet Propulsion Laboratory.

From *Latent Being* to Latent Cinema

On 23 November 2019, RAS launched *Latent Being* – a site-specific, immersive art experience in a former East Berlin power plant called Kraftwerk. For this debut solo exhibition in Germany, we transformed the cathedral-like, vast concrete space of Kraftwerk into a dynamic, temporary, interactive human–AI ecosystem that operated on biofeedback technology. Ten million publicly available visuals as well as sonic and architectural memories of the city were processed through machine-learning algorithms. The installation's interactive component invited the audience to submerge themselves into this synaesthetic cinema experience by simply moving in this historically, culturally and architecturally palimpsest space.

Perception of space – whether it is physical, digital, topological, quantum or hyper – requires various kinds of interactive and cognitive processes through which the audience becomes aware of the relative positions of the *things* around them. Our techno-aesthetic inquiries into how the human mind makes sense of spaces focus on the symbiotic relationship between architecture, neuroscience, technology and machine learning. Stretching beyond a linear understanding of time, movement and causality, *Latent Being* suggested a new sense of space-making through architectural narratives.

Central to the artwork was the ingestion of vast amounts of Berlin-related digital data, like the radical and fully immersive data visualisations of digitised collective memories that were accomplished in the *Infinity Room* series (begun 2015) and in *Machine Hallucination: NYC*. In all three works, cities and urban architectures served as rich sources of narrative inspiration as countless iconic urban locations were treated as if they were living organisms with multiple layers of history and sensation projected on them. Thus, 'data poetics' became a recurrent phrase and a seemingly incongruous way to describe the machine's espousal of the lyrical yet objectified traces of human memories, such as photographs, maps, documents and recorded sounds.

'Connecting with an audience is the point of any story. The question is, how? And how do you know when you've done it?' asks digital anthropologist Frank Rose in his 2021 book *The Sea We Swim In: How Stories Work in a Data-Driven World*.[3] In *Latent Being*, different from our earlier works in the same vein, interactivity took the project to an unprecedented level of theatrical and poetic representation. As the audience found themselves walking through abstract representations of the AI's neural networks, the machine simultaneously learnt about the elements that made up the building's form – not just its physical structure, but also the life inside it. Visitors were observed and became physically connected to the artificial neural process. Eventually, the constant data input – representations of movement, social interactions and space – got transformed into a hallucinogenic large-scale LED screen painting. The artwork was accompanied by a sound piece based on AI-processed field recordings of Berlin also found on the internet.

What visitors of Kraftwerk contributed to was the artwork's continuity, its constantly unfolding narrative in time, representing the ways in which effective human–machine interactions might play a role in shaping the future. The visitors were provided with a tracking device as part of the exhibition. The machine collected location data in addition to recording the amount of time each visitor spent in the installation space. This data, in turn, changed the pace and shape of the AI cinema narrative which the audience was watching and manipulating. The controversial use of the word 'narrative' in relation to an immersive work emerging from a database – a cultural form that represents the world as a list of items without obeying any cause-and-

effect trajectory – is intentional. If, as media archaeologist Lev Manovich suggests, both data and narrative 'claim an exclusive right to make meaning of the world',[4] in their respective ways, the intention in *Latent Being* was to speculate what consciousness and perception of space might mean in a post-digital world.

Architecture as Narrative

The principal architectural statement of *Latent Being* depended on its aesthetic and cinematic qualities, mainly the ways in which the city's, the building's and the visitor's collective memories merged in the mind of a machine to achieve an example of 'synaesthetic cinema through multiple superimpositions'.[5] In addition to evoking a sense of dynamic and expanded consciousness with its strong emphasis on multiplication of spaces and times, the installation pioneered a cinematic storytelling innovation that resulted in an audio-visual, decentred and disorienting space. Following Manovich's theorisation of 'narrative as network', this space could be defined as a fluid architectural sensation where 'a simultaneous flattening and deepening of narrative' took place, turning the interactive installation into an incessant storytelling machine based on unbroken data inflow. 'On the one hand, a narrative is "flattened" into a database. A trajectory through events and/or time becomes a flat space. On the other hand, a flat space of architecture or topology is narrativized, becoming a support for individual users' trajectories.'[6] The idea of narrativising architecture was one of the main elements of the artwork. Equally important was the process through which the audience became part of the narrative by

Refik Anadol Studio,
Latent Being,
Kraftwerk,
Berlin,
2019–20

right: The Kraftwerk building acts as a symbol of a larger narrative which Anadol explores, reminding us that our relationships with other minds – human or artificial – are what we make of them.

opposite: As the machine processes the gigantic visual dataset using the VGG16 neural network, an ocean of images, light and layers of neurons fills the space.

being simultaneously exposed to a hallucinatory level of fragmentation and an expanding (yet enclosed) network of unimaginable connections. Thus, their unpredictable (yet trackable) movements became emblematic of this productive tension, furthering the artwork's central theme about the multi-directionality of collective history.

In his 2001 article 'Towards an Immersive Intelligence', Joseph Nechvatal defined immersive art as 'positing itself as a meta-symbol of and for expanded human potential', because 'aesthetic immersion is about simulation of our internal perceptual circuitry through excess'.[7] *Latent Being* was designed as a space of contemplation where such excess was multi-directional, like the memory itself. A significant feature that public data and stories share is the fact that they do not belong to anyone – they either have to be embedded into a context or projected onto one in order to gain meaning. That context, for *Latent Being*, emerged within the virtual, latent, multidimensional space between the moving body, static architecture and ever-changing intensity of light.

In this way, the Kraftwerk building acted as a symbol for another, larger narrative that the studio explored, namely the transformation of light into meaning with the help of machine intelligence. While the dominant narratives concerning AI in our society tend towards a rather reductive model in which the machine-mind becomes a slave to the human-mind for the advancement of human life only, both 'Machine Hallucinations' and *Latent Being* speculate a subversive narrative of collaboration which, in the long run, might bestow more meaning on how humans connect with their various physical environments.

Latent Being was also a speculation of how the digital age was changing the way we tell visual stories in architectural spaces. The subtitle of Frank Rose's 2012 book on new media and immersive narratives, *The Art of Immersion*, is 'How the Digital Generation Is Changing Hollywood, Madison Avenue, and the Way We Tell Stories'.[8] The list of changing entities that he uses is interesting, as it starts with real (and metonymic) place names and ends with storytelling. It almost indicates that the digital generation changes spaces and institutions in order to change how we tell stories *in* them and *for* them. This is precisely what I seek to uncover by making buildings, institutions and cities tell their own stories with the help of an artificial mind that has the capacity to make connections between memories (data points) in the form of immersive and site-specific visual narratives. ᴆ

This article was written with the research support of Pelin Kivrak, Senior Researcher of Refik Anadol Studio.

Notes
1. Susan Lord and Janine Marchessault, *Fluid Screens, Expanded Cinema*, University of Toronto Press (Toronto), 2008, p 27.
2. Anil Seth, 'What In The World Is Consciousness?', *ScienceNordic*, 26 October 2018: https://sciencenordic.com/biology-denmark-forskerzonen/what-in-the-world-is-consciousness/1459648.
3. Frank Rose, *The Sea We Swim In: How Stories Work in a Data-Driven World*, Norton (New York), 2021, p 45.
4. Lev Manovich, *The Language of New Media*, MIT Press (Cambridge, MA), 2005, p 225.
5. Gene Youngblood, *Expanded Cinema*, Studio Vista (London), 1970, p 111.
6. Manovich, *op cit*, p 284.
7. Joseph Nechvatal, 'Towards an Immersive Intelligence', *Leonardo* 34 (5), 2001, p 418.
8. Frank Rose, *The Art of Immersion: How the Digital Generation Is Remaking Hollywood, Madison Avenue, and the Way We Tell Stories*, WW Norton (New York), 2012.

Strange, But Familiar Enough

The Design Ecology of Neural Architecture

SPAN (Matias del Campo and Sandra Manninger), Robot Garden, Ford Motor Company Robotics Building, University of Michigan, Ann Arbor, Michigan, 2020

After almost a year of conversations and experiments, the University of Michigan Robotics Institute offered SPAN the chance to design the Robot Garden based on 2D-to-3D style transfer techniques geared towards architectural design. The garden is a testing facility for robots. Michigan Robotics has specialised in exploring the possibilities of bipedal robots.

Co-founders and principals of architecture firm SPAN and architectural academics based at the University of Michigan, **Matias del Campo and Sandra Manninger** describe how they became aware of AI technology, setting out some key collaborations, familiarising us with the concept of 'defamiliarisation' and introducing us to some of SPAN's explorations in AI and architecture.

It all started in Vienna in 1998. Sitting in the court of the Baroque ensemble housing the Austrian Institute of Artificial Intelligence (OFAI), SPAN debated the implementation of AI in architecture with OFAI director Robert Trappl and PhD student Arthur Flexer. Fast forward 20 years. In 2018, SPAN received a request from Jessy Grizzle, director of the University of Michigan Robotics Institute: 'Can you design a Robot Garden?' This marked a milestone in SPAN's efforts to design architecture with AI. The collaboration with the university's Robotics and Computer Science departments paved the way to a series of design methods based on various neural networks.

After these first modest efforts, some crucial questions emerged about the being, becoming and reality of this architecture design methodology. Questions about agency, authorship and sensibility in a posthuman design ecology. What is the architect's role in a context where the sole authorship is not in the human anymore but when agency is shared? Can neural networks provoke a novel sensibility in architecture? These questions helped in the critical interrogation of designs embedded in a world increasingly entangled with the various aspects of AI. They provided the bedrock for the ontology of neural architecture. Considering this, the present article focuses on two issues that need discussion in this new ecology of design: *interpolation* and *defamiliarisation*.

The Tricky Nature of Interpolation
In a 2018 lecture,[1] Demis Hassabis, CEO of DeepMind, described the Go game between the AI AlphaGO and nine-dan Go master Lee Sedol, providing a remarkable forensic account of this watershed moment in March 2016 when an AI beat a professional Go player for the first time. Hassabis attempted to answer the question of whether AlphaGo was creative. AlphaGo is at its core a computer program consisting of a sophisticated search tree and several deep neural networks.

A critical aspect of AlphaGO – which resonates in some elements of SPAN's architectural designs, such as the Robot Garden (2020) and House Alpha (2020)
is its ability to learn. AlphaGo, in this instance, is just a stand-in for a massive bulk of neural networks designed to learn, although science is not even entirely sure how human learning works. It learned to play Go by sparring with human players. In time, it was set to play against itself, and it studied thousands of games shared online by amateurs. Ultimately it trained by playing several million examples of GO games. In the second game of the match against Lee Sedol,[2] it made the – now famous – move 37. Lee's facial expression when it dawned on him that there was no way to win this game after move 37 was priceless. A combination of despair, disbelief and pure astonishment.

Hassabis, discussing whether move 37 was indeed creative, laid out three main categories of creativity to make his argument: interpolation, extrapolation and invention. Machines can do well when interpolating between existing data points, meaning that they can create seemingly novel content out of existing information. Extrapolation, on the other hand, is a profoundly human ability. Hassabis further explained that the most challenging aspect to achieve is actual invention. Mainly because the human mind is a massive remixer,[3] constantly pulling up existing knowledge and reassembling it. Resulting in things that might appear novel, but in fact are just the reassembly of existing data. Actual invention poses the problem to the human mind of missing reference points; thus, it is challenging for the mind to recognise genuine innovation because it lacks the means to understand or even perceive it.

SPAN has previously posed the question of whether humans would be able to perceive cultural artefacts created by artificial intelligence.[4] Think of infrared paintings, ultrasound concerts, or poems recited in the speed of light – just a poor attempt to describe and illustrate a culture we as humans might not understand. What those artefacts that neural networks produce undeniably possess is the ability to push the perspective, the field of vision, triggered by the *otherness* of the resulting interpolated artefacts. How then does interpolation relate to extrapolation in this context? Are AIs creative? This seems to be a moot point. It appears more likely that we humans interpret an image produced by a neural network *creatively* rather than the machine being creative.[5]

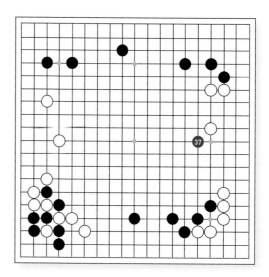

Matias del Campo,
Diagram of AlphaGO's Move 37,
2021

The meaning of this move – performed by the AI AlphaGO at a Go match in March 2016 and marking the first time when a professional Go player was beaten by a computer program – is still debated. Is it proof of creative intention? Or rather the result of a highly trained neural network?

Defamiliarisation

Defamiliarisation, or *ostranenie*, is an alluring area of consideration regarding the discussion of architecture designed with the aid of neural networks. The term itself was coined in 1917. The Russian formalist Viktor Shklovsky described an artistic technique that provoked the audience with imagery depicting everyday things in unfamiliar or strange ways.[6] The goal was to provide the audience with the opportunity to gain new perspectives and observe the world through a different lens, through techniques that introduce abstraction into the aesthetics of realism. Shklovsky suggested that art extends attention; thus slowing down and amplifying assiduity is in itself an aesthetic experience.

More recently, computer scientist and Adobe researcher Aaron Hertzmann, reflecting on some arguments made by the artist Robert Pepperell, identified 'visual indeterminacy' as a crucial feature in what he calls 'GAN art'.[7] These features include a certain amount of realism and coherence in combination with distortions beyond mutation, withstanding a complete interpretation as a consistent form. Thus, the image allows for continuous examination resulting in extended attention. Considering this visual indeterminacy takes place when 'seemingly meaningful visual stimulus that denies easy or immediate identification',[8] it can furthermore be described as the 'lack but promise of semantic stability'.[9]

In this respect, defamiliarisation and estrangement offer the opportunity to observe the world differently than it is commonly understood or perceived.[10] The philosopher Jacques Derrida operates in a similar vein with his thoughts on *différance*.[11] The aspects of defamiliarisation offer a reason why humans respond almost viscerally to images produced by neural networks: these visuals' ability to be strange yet familiar enough for us to recognise them as discernible objects – examples of visual indeterminacy.

Just think, for example, of the work of architects such as Daniel Bolojan, Immanuel Koh and Kyle Steinfeld, or of the creations of the German artist and self-proclaimed neurographer Mario Klingemann: strange, distorted human figures with grotesque bodies, and heads with three eyes, two noses and two sets of mouths. Francis Bacon comes to mind, but in contrast to the visceral artistic will of Bacon, Klingemann's imagery is the result of the inner workings of a generative adversarial network (GAN) operating on the fringes of curve fitting. Klingemann's artworks devour large datasets of historical paintings, primarily portraits, and crunch the data through powerful graphics processing units (GPUs) that produce latent walks through these collections of historic artworks resulting in provocative pieces, such as *Memories of Passersby I* (2018) or *The Butcher's Son* (2017). This is precisely where SPAN chimes in. Intentionally mining the history of architecture and its vast repository of imagery, the oeuvre seeks to tease strange visuals from neural networks and GANs to inspire architectural design – providing surprising, intense, wonderfully weird imagery, fully embedded in a novel aesthetic.

Mario Klingemann,
The Butcher's Son,
'Imposture' series,
2017

above: Artworks like this provoke a discussion on aspects of defamiliarisation. The human figure is distorted, reduced to a grotesquely deformed chunk, a strange 21st-century version of the ancient Roman Belvedere torso.

SPAN (Matias del Campo and Sandra Manninger),
Urban Fictions,
2019

left: A latent walk through a dataset that combines satellite imagery with renderings of 3D modelled patterns resulting in strange urban aggregations.

Machines Hallucinating Architecture

Artificial neural networks are ubiquitous across disciplines due to their high performance in modelling the real world to execute complex tasks in the wild. SPAN's Robot Garden project contains a computational design approach that uses the learned, internal representations of deep-vision neural networks to invoke stylistic edits in both 2D objects (images) and 3D objects (meshes). Positioned along the concave western façade of the new Ford Motor Company Robotics Building at the University of Michigan, the garden serves as a testing ground for mobile robots of various families.

The garden's design is entirely based on a GAN and neural style transfer, using AI in all steps of the design process. This method made it possible to design a synthetic ecology oscillating between the natural and the artificial. The resulting digital model provided the template for the construction, and it continues to serve the purpose of simulating and preparing the testing of robots in the garden. The garden itself is executed in natural materials, providing different terrains such as grass, gravel, stone, sand and water, and topographical features, inclinations and pits to emulate rugged terrain. The site provided was analysed using a set of satellite images as a basis. The given shape of the area was cut out of the satellite images to create a set of pictures geared towards 2D-to-3D neural mesh rendering. In an attempt to have a neural network dream or hallucinate architectural features on the site, it was trained using an extensive library of images of columns, stairs and fountains. Surprisingly the

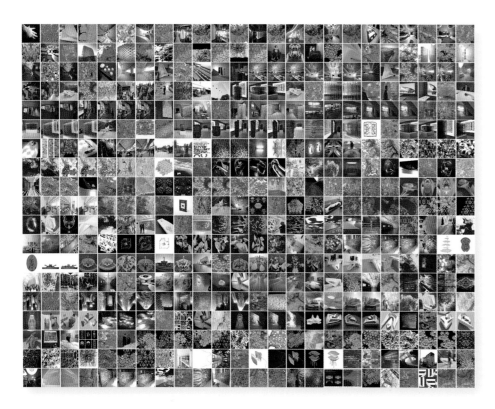

SPAN (Matias del Campo and Sandra Manninger),
Latent SPAN, 2020

Snapshot of the dataset of images put together from the archives of SPAN. These images represent a small section of a dataset of several thousand images created by SPAN between 2010 and 2020.

SPAN (Matias del Campo
and Sandra Manninger),
Latent SPAN,
2020

Latent walk through a dataset of
the work of SPAN. It is clear that the
resulting images are an interpolation
of existing datapoints. A neural
network can thus interrogate the
work through a different lens than
the original author.

SPAN (Matias del Campo
and Sandra Manninger),
Robot Garden,
Ford Motor Company
Robotics Building,
University of Michigan,
Ann Arbor, Michigan,
2020

One of the glitchy results of the
first attempts to convert a 3D image
into a 3D model. Various methods
were tested such as 2D-to-3D style
transfer, 3D-to-3D style transfer
and bump mapping. The, at
times, strange results served as a
template for further development.

SPAN (Matias del Campo
and Sandra Manninger),
24 Highschool,
Shenzhen, China,
2020

The project was generated using a novel
method: employing language to dictate the
basic features (plus some provocations)
to an attentional generative adversarial
network (AttnGAN) in order to produce
the images that served as its foundation.

resulting images represent a novel view of these archaic architectural features. The hybrid nature of the resulting meshes means they do not show the features in total clarity but are rather the hallucinogenic dream of a machine trying to see these features in the landscape.

Language as a Design Driver

The motivation to explore attentional generative adversarial networks (AttnGAN) as a design technique in architecture can be found in the desire to interrogate an alternative design methodology that relies not on images but on language as a starting point for architectural design. Traditionally architectural design depends on visual language to initiate a design process, whether a napkin sketch or a quick doodle in a 3D modelling environment. AttnGAN explores the information space present in programmatic needs, expressed in written form, and transforms them into a visual output. This visual output can be further processed into three-dimensional models that transport lingual information into fully developed architectural entities. The key results of this research are demonstrated in a proof-of-concept project: the 2020 competition entry for the 24 Highschool in Shenzhen, China. This award-winning project demonstrated the ability of AttnGAN to serve as a successful design methodology for a reasonably complex architecture programme. In the area of neural architecture, this technique allows shape to be interrogated through language: an alternative design method that creates its own unique sensibility.

GraphCNN as a Design Method

Exploring machine-learning methods allows us to interrogate large datasets of architectural archetypes based solely on 3D models instead of 2D representations. SPAN's House Alpha proposition uses a flexible dataset structure called a graph. It utilises the generalisation of the standard convolutional neural network (CNN), called graph convolutional neural network (GCNN), to model and perform the entirety of the design process by only applying 3D models and information. The central claim of this idea is to provide a possible solution to the question: How can a neural network interrogate the inherent sensibility of a specific designer? This idea relies on the possibility of modelling a designer's sensibility as a high-dimensional function that can be learned to produce novel design solutions. The backbone of this design technique is GCNNs, which are capable of modelling both the perception and creation of architectural objects. The key is to train a GCNN to capture a specific designer's aesthetic sensibilities based on neuroaesthetic labels, such as primary visual features (eg coloration, geometric features like scale, and semantic properties), aesthetic quality and functional quality. To train a neural network to generatively create new 3D models based on the design sensibility of a specific designer, it is necessary to collect a dataset of models that were organically modelled by that designer.

Folding the Wicked and the Tame Together

The previous examples demonstrate the ability of neural networks to provide design methods able to extract information from any given dataset. In so doing, they enrich the architect's design ecology, covering a wide range of possibilities from morphological and aesthetical studies to pragmatic problem solving. The next step to come after this first wave of experimental projects is the implementation of improved datasets, created specifically for architectural design. This will allow the presented design methods to improve by folding the wicked and the tame problem into a holistic approach to AI design in architecture. ⌂

Notes
1. Demis Hassabis, 'Creativity and AI', The Rothschild Foundation Lecture, Royal Academy of Arts, London, 17 September 2018: https://youtu.be/d-bvsJWmqlc.
2. Google DeepMind Challenge Match, Seoul, South Korea, 9–15 March 2016: https://deepmind.com/alphago-korea.
3. See University of Haifa. 'How Does Our Brain Form Creative and Original Ideas?', *ScienceDaily*, 19 November 2015: www.sciencedaily.com/releases/2015/11/151119104105.htm.
4. See Matias del Campo and Sandra Manninger. 'The Church of AI: An Examination of Architecture in a Posthuman Design Ecology', in Matthias Hank Haeusler *et al* (eds), *Proceedings of the 24th CAADRIA Conference – Volume 2*, Victoria University of Wellington (Wellington), 2019, pp 767–72.
5. See Anton Oleinik, 'What Are Neural Networks Not Good At? On Artificial Creativity', *Big Data and Society* 6 (1), January 2019.
6. Viktor Shklovsky, 'Art as Device', in *Theory of Prose*, Kalkey Archive Press (London), 1991, pp 1–14.
7. Aaron Hertzmann, 'Visual Indeterminacy in Generative Neural Art', *Leonardo* 53 (4), 2020: ArXiv:1910.04639 (2019).
8. Dario Gamboni, *Potential Images: Ambiguity and Indeterminacy in Modern Art*, Reaktion Books (London), 2004, pp 57–63.
9. Ernst Gombrich, *Art and Illusion: A Study in the Psychology of Pictorial Representation*, Princeton University Press (Princeton, NJ), 1960, pp 122–36.
10. See Michael Young, 'The Affects of Realism – Or the Estrangement of the Background', in Matias del Campo (ed), ⌂ *Evoking Through Design: Contemporary Moods in Architecture*, November/December (no 6), 2016, p 60.
11. See Lawrence Crawford, 'Viktor Shklovskij: Différance in Defamiliarization', *Comparative Literature* 36 (3), 1984, pp 209–19.

Hannah Daugherty, Marianna Moreira
de Calvahro and Imman Suleiman,
Augmented, thesis project,
Taubman College of Architecture
and Urban Planning,
University of Michigan,
Ann Arbor, Michigan,
2019

'Deep dreaming' is a good example of how engineers have borrowed terms from psychology and neuroscience. However, care has to be taken relative to the mechanics of algorithms. Nonexperts tend to compare terms like 'dreaming' and 'hallucinating' to the human experience, yet the translation into an algorithm is only inspired by these neurological processes, not a perfect copy of them. Thus ANNs are closer to parameter tuning in order to extract the desired information, which is described as 'learning'.

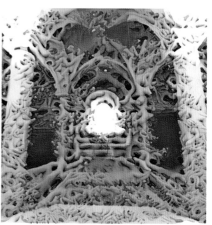

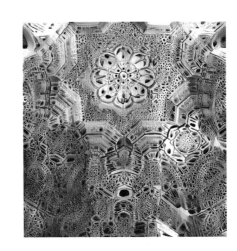

Matias del Campo

In Conversation with Alexandra Carlson

WHEN ROBOTS DREAM

Matias del Campo interviews **Alexandra Carlson** who had a key role in founding the pioneering Architecture and Artificial Intelligence Laboratory (AR²IL) at the University of Michigan's Robotics Department and Taubman College of Architecture and Urban Planning. The synthesis of the architectural and dataset sharing adds another dimension to design possibilities.

With a neuroscience background and a PhD in Robotics, Alexandra Carlson developed an interest in the interdisciplinary nature of applying machine learning techniques to architectural design. In joining the University of Michigan's Architecture and Artificial Intelligence Laboratory (AR²IL) in 2018 as advisor and tutor to design studios, she embarked on a collaboration during which specific questions and aspects started to emerge that are still being discussed ferociously in the discipline right now – questions about agency, creativity, authorship, ethics and aesthetics of AI in architecture. In the August 2021 interview that forms the basis of this article, she explored her thoughts on several key theoretical aspects of this emerging field.

Final reviews,
Imagining the Real - Architecture in
the Age of Automation thesis studio,
Taubman College of Architecture
and Urban Planning,
University of Michigan,
Ann Arbor, Michigan,
April 2019

Alexandra Carlson contributed to the studio's knowledge base by teaching students how to set up and prepare neural networks for machine-learning tasks. This was one of the first studios dedicated entirely to AI methods in architectural design.

Are Neural Networks Creative?

The conversation about artificial neural networks (ANNs), and more specifically about generative adversarial networks (GANs) and convolutional neural networks (CNNs), instantly provokes questions about the interrogation of creativity within the human realm and the ability to synthetically replicate it with an algorithm, as well as creative culture at large. As Carlson puts it: 'When defining creativity, you have to think about what it means to be novel. It's not just something never seen before; it is about producing something that is more than the sum of its parts. It is very much aligned along thoughts about neural networks' ability to interpolate versus extrapolate.'

Interpolation is the estimation of new data points, or features, *within* a range of a discrete set of known data points. Extrapolation, on the other hand, estimates features that exist *outside* the range of known features captured in or defined by a dataset; the algorithm in question must understand the relationships between data points to such a deep level that it can then estimate unseen/unobserved features outside the range of the training data.

Deep neural networks (DNNs) are designed for interpolation.[1] When applied to image datasets, these algorithms can not only extract useful and salient features that mimic what we see in the primary visual cortex of the human brain,[2] but also generate images that contain novel combinations of these features. This ability has been used to generate incredible and alien images using deep dreaming, neural style transfer and GANs.

GANs, in particular, are an excellent example of dataset interpolation: they learn the distribution of different types of visual features and how they covary in the real world.[3] Thus, we can sample this distribution, which is where all the exciting and unique, never-before-seen combinations exist. However, these algorithms, as well as ANNs in general, are not able to reason about or generate features for regions of the visual feature space where no training data is available. Thus, a neural network cannot reliably extrapolate to new, unseen data regimes. In Carlson's words, 'They miss the requirement of being able to extrapolate and thus of being creative as to how we observe that process as it manifests in humans.'

Alexandra Carlson,
Neural style transfer between
a 19th-century science plate of
the moon and Nolli maps of Rome,
2019

The main ability of neural networks to perform interpolations allows them to extract useful and salient features that mimic what is seen in the primary visual cortex of the human brain. However, they can also generate images that contain novel/unseen combinations of these features. This example shows a neural style transfer between a 19th-century science plate of the moon and Nolli maps of Rome: suddenly there is a city on the moon.

Complex Biology and Simple Machines

Carlson believes that this discussion of the limits of artificial creativity in the context of human creativity could also have roots in the differing levels of complexity between biological neural networks (BNNs) versus ANNs. The ability of ANNs to mimic different aspects of the human design process is constrained by how they learn and process data.

The biggest difference between BNNs and ANNs is how time influences information processing. ANNs, primarily the ones that are used in supervised vision tasks, do not capture time in the way they integrate information. In ANNs, there are weight values that are associated with each connection between each neuron. Each of these weights filters incoming information and transmits it to the neurons in the next layer. However, this information processing is static; time is not encoded into the information as it moves through the network. We train artificial neural networks offline on large datasets, fix their weights, and then apply/deploy them to the real world in the hope that we have trained them well enough to be able to generalise to new situations.[4]

SPAN (Matias del Campo and Sandra Manninger),
Robot Garden,
Ford Motor Company Robotics Building,
University of Michigan, Ann Arbor, Michigan,
2020

The Robot Garden project afforded the opportunity to explore an entire series of neural-network-based design methods – from deep dreaming, based on features of fountains, columns and arches, to neural style transfer to define the various landscaping features: sand, rocks, gravel and earth. The resulting images were then transformed into 3D models using depth mapping.

In a biological brain, a neuron cell will integrate incoming information in the form of little ion channels opening up and ions flowing into the cell

The AR²IL is a project dedicated to developing a variety of different techniques that derive from machine learning and machine vision to aid in the entire architecture design process. It is no longer about the design of a building; we can do design on a variety of scales, from furniture to cities.

ANNs, when they first came to fruition, were meant to be an algorithmic description of network behaviour in the human brain.[5] In a biological brain, a neuron cell will integrate incoming information in the form of little ion channels opening up and ions flowing into the cell. If the concentration of ions surpasses a certain threshold in a given time period, an electric spike is produced (indicating the presence of a feature) that is then sent to other downstream cells. The way that time is used in the human brain is fundamental and inherent to how information is actually represented and processed; feature information is literally encoded in the temporal properties of the outgoing signal of electric spikes.[6] Furthermore, biological neurons are not restricted to only have feedforward connections, as ANNs are. They can transmit information to any part of the network, both forwards and backwards in terms of information flow, allowing for significantly more network activity states and thus more complexity in information processing.

As neuroscience has progressed, especially in the last several years, it has become very apparent that the way that biological neurons actually integrate information is exceptionally more complex than the simple artificial neuron models that we currently have at our disposal. For example, there is evidence that the anatomical structures that bring information into the neuron cell body, called dendrites, perform computation in their appendages before information even reaches the cell body.[7] This complex, dynamic spatiotemporal behaviour is difficult to model and is something that we have not been able to capture with the static artificial neurons we have today.

SPAN (Matias del Campo and Sandra Manninger),
Grid of a Baroque plan dataset composed of
scraped images from the internet,
2020

Regardless of how state-of-the-art a network is, if the dataset does not contain the needed information, the network will not learn to perform according to the requirements. Responding to this problem, the AR²IL embarked on creating their own datasets ensuring that the necessary information exists within them. The goal is to explore what is really the design power of artificial neural networks (ANNs). How much of the design process can we automate with these algorithms?

The biggest achievement for the AR²IL lab is bringing the idea of data and data sharing into the architectural realm

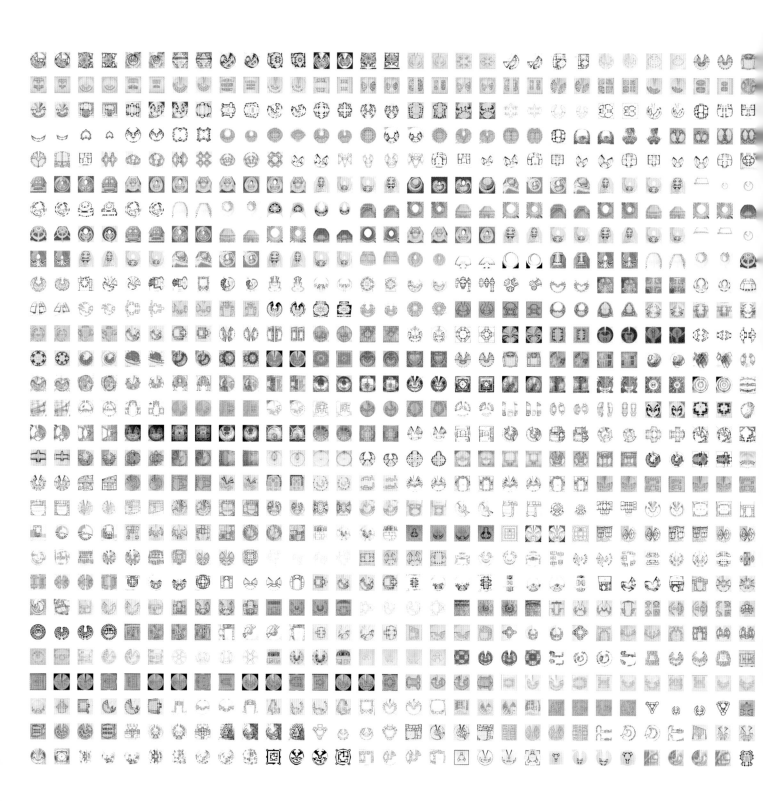

From Analysis to Design Generation

What is happening in the AR²IL is a project in terms of developing a variety of different techniques that derive from machine vision to aid in the entire design process. Currently, the research is moving from the first phase of experimentation in which 'found data' was used (typically off the internet), to the conscious and focused creation of datasets specifically tailored towards architectural design, emphasising the use of neural networks both analytically as well as generatively.

Carlson observes, 'We started off by really just exploring what was possible with the machine vision algorithms that existed. One of the interesting questions was whether it is possible to create an artificial design process. The first step to answering this question is to collect a lot more data. In particular, data that was organically made by architects.' To date, most of the data being dealt with was created by non-experts, meaning: not by architects. The problem is that to algorithmically capture the design process, accurate information is needed – data that contains information about the design process – which currently is not the case. 'There is only so much that different neural architectures can achieve, whether they are of the ANN or computational BNN families, and this is true across most computer-vision tasks. The network can be the most state-of-the-art, high-performing algorithm possible, but if you have a dataset that doesn't actually contain the information relevant to the task, then the networks are not going to learn to perform in the way that you want them to. As a result of this problem, we embarked on creating our own datasets where we can guarantee that this information exists within them, and then use them to start exploring what is really the design power.'

The biggest achievement for the AR²IL lab is bringing the idea of data and data sharing into the architectural realm. One of the largest differences between the disciplines of architecture and computer science is the sense of sharing information. With this idea of large, shared datasets that multiple people can access and use to explore various novel design processes, we are on the trajectory to really changing the approach, the idea of experimentation within the field in general. As Carlson concludes, 'we are really trying to bring about the emergence of a new mindset in architecture'. ᴆ

This article is based on a Zoom meeting between Matias del Campo and Alexandra Carlson on 15 August 2021.

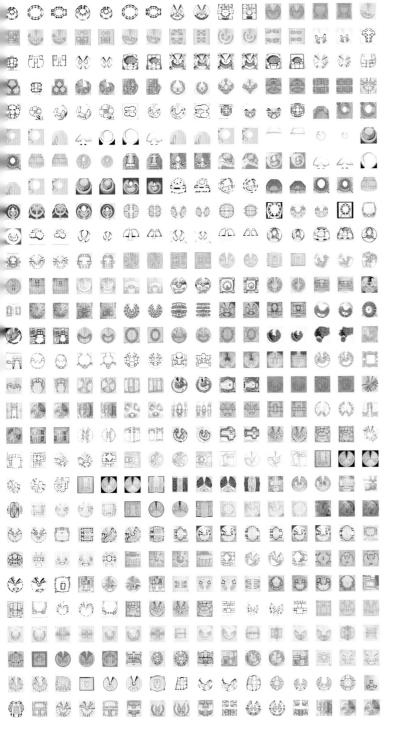

Notes
1. H Lohninger, *Fundamentals of Statistics*: www.statistics4u.com/fundstat_eng/.
2. See Chelsea Voss *et al*, 'Visualizing Weights', *Distill* 6 (2), 2021: e00024-007 and Alex Krizhevsky, Ilya Sutskever and Geoffrey E Hinton, 'Imagenet Classification with Deep Convolutional Neural Networks', *Advances in Neural Information Processing Systems* 25, 2012, pp 1097–1105.
3. See Ian Goodfellow, Yoshua Bengio and Aaron Courville, *Deep Learning*, MIT Press (Cambridge, MA), 2016, pp 143–56.
4. *Ibid*.
5. See Warren S McCulloch and Walter Pitts, 'A Logical Calculus of Ideas Immanent in Nervous Activity', *Bulletin of Mathematical Biophysics* 5 (4), 1943, pp 115–33.
6. See Eugene M Izhikevich, *Dynamical Systems in Neuroscience*, MIT Press (Cambridge, MA), 2007, pp 67–74.
7. See Hongbo Jia *et al*, 'Dendritic Organization of Sensory Input to Cortical Neurons In Vivo', *Nature* 464 (7293), 2010, pp 1307–12 and Tiago Branco, Beverley A Clark and Michael Häusser, 'Dendritic Discrimination of Temporal Input Sequences in Cortical Neurons', *Science* 329 (5999), 2010, pp 1671–5.

Sofia Crespo and Feileacan McCormick

Augmenting Digital Nature

Generative Art as a Constructive Feedback Loop

Sofia Crespo and Feileacan McCormick use AI in their generative artworks. They are interested in natural ecology, biology and the way organisms adapt and evolve in relationship to their environment. The augmentation of their own creativity by AI helps them process complicated, unsolvable 'wicked' problems and produces some stunningly beautiful art along the way.

Sofia Crespo, ((Opening _the_Ocean's_Heart)), 'Neural Zoo' series, 2018

A neural networks exploration of a dataset leads to new ways of seeing and understanding the natural world. Akin to a view through a microscope, what we see are patterns not normally readily visible to us.

Can you imagine a colour that you have never seen before? Try as you may, ultimately it is the sum of your experiences, the 'dataset' of your existence that determines what you can imagine. The boundaries of your imagination are sculpted from your perceptions of the world.

At Entangled Others Studio, the more we focus upon the topic of ecology through our artistic practice, the more we have begun to see that all of us need more than our lived experiences if we are to be able to adapt to the radical reshaping of our world that we are already living. It could be said we face a crisis of imagination. One way of viewing change is as an acknowledgement of the hitherto unknown, that way of framing or engaging with others that quickly becomes mundane. How do we expand the imaginative horizon to be able to recognise new possible ways of being when they emerge, rather than staying in the tunnel vision of the now?

Sofia Crespo,
{Organic_resonance_9867},
'Neural Zoo' series,
2019

The vivid digital distillation of a coral reef carries within it a promise of coherence, yet constantly dissolves and shifts as the eye travels across the image.

Digitised Boundaries of Imagination

AI, or rather, artificial neural networks (ANNs), are modelled to mimic aspects of our cognition. They tend to distil their learnings into an 'essence', much as our brains do: to train a neural network is to accept the loss of data to extract some key patterns that can somehow manage to represent the essential qualities of, say, a jellyfish or a flower. An example is a visual network that first learns edges and lines from a dataset of images; from these it then forms an understanding of common low-level features – for example, eyes and noses – and finally high-level features such as full faces.

The resulting model contains within it the sum of these distilled understandings, often referred to as a space that can be sampled at various coordinates to extract knowledge. The latent space of a majority of artificial neural network models trained upon what many perceive as a benchmark dataset, such as ImageNet,[1] can be seen as a distilled mundane space. Most models trained on datasets that have their origin in publicly available data or data scraped from online sources can be considered to be mundane in that they represent the common extents of people's worldview and its contents, albeit somewhat problematically at times.[2] Latent spaces are therefore very much mundane spaces.

This applies equally to all applications of neural networks. As humanity attempts to interact more deeply with its context, there is a greater need for novel, purpose-made datasets that contain the many additional layers of metadata and meaning encoded into our reality. Even then the model space will still be a mirror of the mundane, yet the modern context it is created for is changing faster than ever. Humanity's current approach risks the creation of neural networks whose resulting models are unable to engage productively with our new reality of 'there is no new normal'.[3] As artists, rather than resign ourselves to this, we can explore how alternative framings can be part of the creative practice.

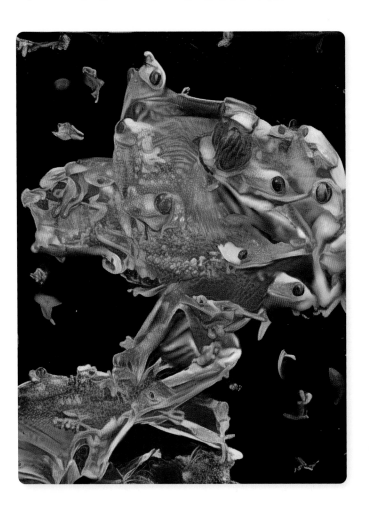

Sofia Crespo,
{Morphing_3234},
'Neural Zoo' series,
2018

Through the lens of a neural network, the camouflage colourings of rainforest frogs take the forms of the very leaves they seek to appear one with, blurring our perception of cross-species boundaries.

The Mundane = Obsolete

The focus upon starting with the mundane is not coincidental. The narrative of infinite growth as well as the distribution of production and consumption in a global infrastructure have disconnected us from local feedback loops that might have otherwise shaped us into a very different trajectory. The model of reality that we have as a base for our daily choices and perceptions has drifted. This widening chasm negatively affects our ability to enact meaningful changes and perceive correctly critical opportunities and choices. The substrate we need to reshape is the mundane, everyday perception.

Naturally, we as artists are biased in that we primarily attempt to engage with these issues through art created with generative tools such as machine learning, also known as AI. We consider AI a tool, just like the microscope which allows what is otherwise invisible to the naked eye to be seen. The generated images of the 'Neural Zoo' series reveal the essential visual qualities that make a person recognise something like a jellyfish. Before continuing, it is prudent to mention that the word 'intelligence' in the term 'artificial intelligence' is misleading as it falsely implies some sort of consciousness and superiority. Popular views generally hold that animals are not intelligent, this being an inherited bias reinforced by cultural narrative, but AI is viewed without that bias as it does not appear to emerge from the natural world, leading people to imbue it with all kinds of hype, hope and dreams.

AI as an Augmentation of the Mind

The boundaries of imagination in the resulting model from any artificial neural network are quite clear: these models cannot directly generate anything outside the contents of the original dataset. As such, their so-called imagination has its clear boundaries, beyond which patterns de-cohere into an intangible visual soup. The manipulation and 'circuit-bending' of these models need to be considered as a means to seize the potential of repurposing their mirroring of mundanity to create hybrid visions and forms that can act as a stepping stone towards seeing and engaging with new future ways of seeing, being and building. AI tools are perhaps more productively viewed as potential augmentations of the mind or 'mental prosthetics' that can be used as a means to expand our imagination of the mundane, rather than as a means to automation of tasks. This view builds on the tradition of generative arts to create at scales and complexities that would be unfeasible otherwise, enabling the exploration of the space that emerges from an initial set of data and algorithmic rules.

In the series 'Hybrid Ecosystems', this approach was adopted to utilise the limited territory of our mundane spaces as a means to reach and engage outwards, without waiting or hesitating. A model trained on everything from humans or aeroplanes to insects and trees can be pushed and prodded to manipulate into generating outputs where the fictitious divide between the digital and physical dissolves and we as viewers encounter visions of hybrid ecosystems where humanity's technologies are harmonious parts of greater ecosystems.

Feileacan McCormick/
Entangled Others Studio,
Data harvest,
'Hybrid Ecosystems' series,
2021

right: If we imagine ecosystems not only as interacting systems, but as symbiotically computational systems, what would the act of reading and writing data look like? Would data be harvested seasonally by certain species, readied for migration?

Feileacan McCormick/
Entangled Others Studio,
Multiplicity engine,
'Hybrid Ecosystems' series,
2021

far right: As we slowly attempt to dissolve the perceived boundary of the physical-digital divide, strange chimeric forms emerge, natural machines powered by engines serving the needs of species other than our own.

Feileacan McCormick /
Entangled Others Studio,
Data migration,
'Hybrid Ecosystems series,
2021

Within the mundane (latent) spaces of neural networks, how can we reimagine digital communication as part of new seasonal cycles, where data migrates at a variety of speeds and instinctive routes?

Due to the nature of generative tools, artists are not limited in terms of outputs, we can produce an endless myriad of variations, alternative takes and new (re)combinations of the mundane. As humans we crave new stimuli and novelty to remain focused. Neural networks as mental prosthetics might just permit us to circumvent the typical limits of capacity, allowing the construction of feedback loops into our creative practice that erode the edges of mundanity.

It would not hurt to consider AI as a cognitive augmentation, one allowing us to remain focused and engaged with the wicked problems we face that human cognition often struggles to even comprehend. These kinds of problems are nigh-impossible to solve due to their complexity and shifting nature, unlike 'tame' problems that are finite and can be easily solved. This augmentation of the mind is not just about enacting a more-than-human meditation upon how we see and represent the world and nonhuman others. By avoiding the techno-optimistic drive towards automation, and instead endeavouring to create feedback loops as part of a personal practice, we stand unable to hide behind any such claims of an objective, platonic decision process: the process, the results and its consequences are firmly entangled with us. As artists, architects and planetary co-inhabitants we are responsible for expanding the collective imagination of a more-than-human future. ⚙

Notes
1. www.image-net.org.
2. See Kate Crawford and Trevor Paglen, 'Excavating AI: The Politics of Images in Machine Learning Training Sets', The AI Now Institute, New York University, 19 September 2019: https://excavating.ai.
3. Tweet by Alex Steffen, 28 July 2018: https://twitter.com/AlexSteffen/status/1023242666182696965.

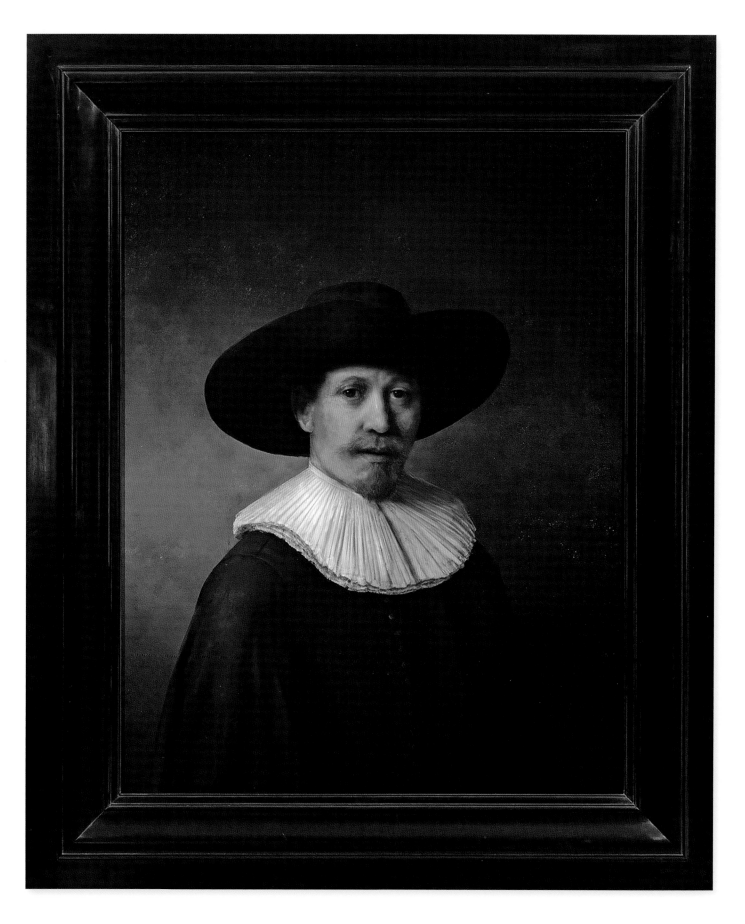

AI & Myths of Creativity

Lev Manovich, Director of the Cultural Analytics Lab and Presidential Professor at the City University of New York, explores some of the societal notions surrounding AI and creativity. He exposes certain myths that have grown up around this discourse and posits a wider, more interesting emerging reality.

Current discussions about the adoption of AI in visual arts, design, architecture, cinema, music and other arts often rely on widely accepted ideas about art and creativity. These include such notions as 'Art is the most creative human domain', 'Artists do not follow rules' and 'Generation of original art is a great test of AI progress'. The goal of this text is to briefly discuss the historical origins of popular ideas about art and creativity, and suggest that they limit our vision of cultural AI.

Art as the Embodiment of Creativity

Our dominant concept of art comes from the Romantic period in Europe: the end of the 19th and first part of the 20th centuries. The idea goes like this: artists are different from normal people. They occupy a special place in society. Their art comes from the inside, from their imagination and not from any rules or examples. It is not a result of rational decisions. Instead it is driven by intuition and it expresses emotions. And, most importantly: art is the exclusive domain of human creativity.[1] (The term 'creative industries' is one example of how the Romantic association of creativity with art is now taken for granted in society.)

The assumptions that art, as opposed to any other field of human activity, best embodies creativity, and also that art is the best expression of human uniqueness, lead to the following seemingly logical conclusion: *the best test of the progress of AI is whether it can generate (novel) art.*

Here we encounter a fascinating paradox. In the 19th and first part of the 20th century, it was still assumed that artists need to train for years to acquire specialised skills in drawing, perspective, composition, etc. But as the ideology of modern art based on Romantic ideas gradually became dominant, the requirement of learning such skills also disappeared.

Since 1970 the contemporary art world has become conceptual, ie focused on ideas. It is no longer about visual skills but semantic skills. Although art now focuses on communicating semantic messages, for a while it still valued Modernist ambiguity and wanted audiences to struggle with interpretations. However, by the start of the 21st century, as contemporary art entered mainstream culture and groups of schoolchildren became frequent museum visitors, art could no longer afford to be 'difficult' or ambiguous. Similarly to how it functioned before the 20th century in the West, today art again serves moral and political functions.

There are only a few art academies in China, Korea and Russia that still systematically teach 19th-century traditional drawing and painting skills. In most art schools and university art departments oriented towards the contemporary art world, students are told to start 'expressing their inner vision' and 'developing their unique style' right away. Instead of art-making skills, they learn the verbal language of contemporary art as it exists in the statements of artists and galleries, and the texts of critics and curators in catalogues and other publications.

To be an artist who belongs (or wants to belong) to the contemporary global art world is to speak and write in this language, rather than to possess any skills in colour combination, composition, drawing, photo and video editing,

3D modelling and animation, computer programming or game design. This ideology also defines how art is viewed in global culture at large. Art can express unique 'artistic visions', or 'play some special role', or 'address social issues', or 'question' dominant social values. But it is not about involving any specialised skills, or creating beauty, or expressing and arousing emotions. These functions have been fully taken over in the 20th century by mass culture such as cinema and popular music – and today also by social media where millions of people showcase their fashion looks, photographs, manga drawings, 3D characters and other creations.

However, semantic art has never completely taken over visual arts. In endless galleries, museums, art websites and social media galleries we continue to see figurative, semi-figurative and abstract images. They do not communicate any obvious linguistic messages. They employ all the visual languages developed in the realist 19th and Modernist 20th centuries, and they can be situated anywhere between realism and abstraction. They do not innovate visually, because after the Modernist century (1870–1970), there is nothing left to invent. (And new effects enabled by Photoshop and other media software in the 1990s have by now become part of the Modernist legacy.)

This kind of visual art is everywhere today, while a more specialised world of contemporary high art is less visible. Most people feel too intimidated to even approach contemporary art museums.

This is why for people who do not have expertise in the art world, contemporary art is equated with 19th-century realism and 20th-century Modernism – ie two-dimensional images that represent something in either a detailed or schematic way. And this is why so much effort in AI research is now devoted to automatically generating images that look either like realistic works from past centuries, or abstract and semi-abstract works from the 20th century (as opposed to, for example, installations, site-specific art projects or other recent types of art). For AI researchers and also the general public, such images are equated with art. That is, their visual similarity to what popular culture labels as 'visual art' is assumed to be sufficient. And this is why the use of AI methods in interactive art or experimental music does not fascinate the news media or the public – because this kind of art is not popular with the general public, unless it is promoted by Google as the latest AI art, or has a purely entertainment function.

Art and Realism

As demonstrated by many research studies in the social sciences, for the majority of people today art indeed means pictures, realism and skills.[2] An artist is understood as a person who has skills to make figurative 2D images, professional-looking photographs, animated 3D models of human figures, manga drawings, and other figurative representations that are hard or impossible to make without a long period of training or practice. Search for 'art' in Instagram or on YouTube, and you will come across endless tutorials, guides and courses on how to acquire such skills.

Lev Manovich / Cultural Analytics Lab,
Phototrails,
University of California, San Diego,
2013

Visualisation of 50,000 images shared on Instagram in Tokyo during spring 2012. The project explored content and styles of photos shared on Instagram in 13 global cities. Using techniques from computer vision (a subfield of AI), the team measured visual properties of 2.3 million photographs and visualised the photos shared in each city sorted by these properties. In this visualisation, the images are sorted by average brightness and colour hue.

The idea of specialised skills that need to be mastered also defines all areas of the culture industry – professional photography, anime and animation, game design, web and interaction design, cinematography, video editing, acting, TV and film directing, music production and so on. Often when professionals from the culture industry are evaluated, the idea of learning skills and achieving technical mastery is combined with the idea of high creativity. For example, if a very successful culture industry professional is referred to as a 'real artist', this assumes that he or she has both superb mastery of the craft and also highly original style and/or content.

This commonly held view of art explains why realistic images, similar to the ones of great artists from the past, that are generated by AI receive the most media attention today. People are very impressed when a research team has used AI to recreate destroyed parts of Rembrandt's *The Night Watch*,[3] or when a student has used AI to create images that look like classical Chinese landscape paintings to the extent that they fooled 55 per cent of participants in an experiment.[4] But an AI that can make abstract art does not make news.

In an experiment conducted by the Data Science Lab at the Institute for Basic Science (IBS) in Daejeon, South Korea in spring 2021, a group of people without any art training were shown both realistic and abstract images, and asked to judge whether each image was made by a human artist or AI. Images which had a significant level of detail were most frequently assumed to be made by human artists, while simple abstract images were assumed to be generated by AI.[5] In reality, all the images in the experiments were generated using a recent StyleGAN2 neural network model that was trained by the scientists on tens of thousands of historical paintings from the wikiart.org site.

Creativity and Global Economy

Yet another relevant idea taken for granted today is a relatively recent one that became popular in the early 2000s. Global competition and easier access to foreign markets as part of economic globalisation have motivated a new paradigm in business. Your company now needs to be 'creative' and it needs to innovate constantly. The global success of Apple and Samsung in the 2000s, based on their innovative strategies, has become an example for all businesses.

The highly influential book of urban theorist Richard Florida, *The Creative Class* (2002), also played an important role. According to Florida, the economic function of this class is 'to create new ideas, new technology and/or creative content'.[6] In his analysis, the creative class already included 30 per cent of the US workforce by the early 2000s.[7] Florida argues that cities that can attract this class will prosper. His work had a big effect. For example, the leaders of Berlin were influenced by his ideas and in the 2000s set up policies to attract professionals in design, software and media from other countries to the city.

Still later, the idea took hold that creativity is highly desirable for society as a whole and individuals in general, and became a new universal social value in the 2010s. Everybody should be creative – and computer technologies

Assem Zhunis and Lev Manovich,
Images generated by StyleGAN2 neural networks
trained on 81,000 paintings from Wikiart.org,
Data Science Lab,
Institute for Basic Science,
Daejeon, South Korea,
2021

These images were used in an experiment where people were asked to guess if each was created by a human artist or an AI. Most responders assumed that realistic images shown in the bottom row came from human artists, while simple abstract images shown in the top row were created by AIs.

Perceived as

AI-Generated

Human-Created

are here to help us. (Which means that we all, to some extent, should become 'artists'.) A new term 'creative technologist' that became popular in the 2010s is an example of these trends.

This idea led to a different assumption – that AI and technology in general should help individuals and companies to be creative and innovative. Now, we no longer want AI to only simulate human cognitive functions such as vision, speech and reasoning, or to quickly search through millions of documents or translate between languages. This was enough in the 20th century – but not the 21st. Now we want AI to generate creative and innovative solutions or help us to do this – because society assumes that creativity is the driver of the economy.

Dissociating AI and Creativity Concepts

All this means that in the future, when our ideas about art, artists and creativity will change (there is no reason why they should stay the same), the link between AI and the arts that now seems obvious may also become weaker or disappear. And this will be a good thing. I am personally looking forward to this. The proportion of creative people in the arts is no different from that in any other field of human activity. Although the templates, examples and tactics used by many contemporary artists, designers, architects and other creatives today may not all be as explicit as Lightroom presets or WordPress themes, they are no less real.

The association of the arts and creativity that we take for granted today, and the privileging of creativity over other considerations, are relatively recent inventions. Thus, rather than obsessing over the question 'Can AI be creative?', we should explore other ideas about what AI can do for art, design, architecture and all other art fields. ∞

Notes
1. See Aidan Day, *Romanticism*, 2nd edn, Routledge (London), 2012.
2. See for instance Roger Batt *et al*, 'Style and Spectral Power: Processing of Abstract and Representational Art in Artists and Non-Artists', *Perception* 39 (12), 2010, pp 1659–71.
3. Cristina Criddle, 'Rembrandt's *The Night Watch* painting restored by AI', BBC News, 23 June 2021: www.bbc.com/news/technology-57588270.
4. Alice Xue, 'End-to-End Chinese Landscape Painting Creation Using Generative Adversarial Networks', 11 November 2020: http://arxiv.org/pdf/2011.05552v1.pdf.
5. Gabriel Lima *et al*, 'On the Social-Relational Moral Standing of AI: An Empirical Study Using AI-Generated Art', *Frontiers in Robotics and AI* 8, August 2021: www.frontiersin.org/articles/10.3389/frobt.2021.719944/full.
6. Richard Florida, *The Rise of the Creative Class: And How It's Transforming Work, Leisure, Community, and Everyday Life*, Perseus Book Group (New York), 2002, p 8.
7. Richard Florida, *The Rise of the Creative Class – Revisited: 10th Anniversary Edition*, Basic Books (New York), 2012, p vii.

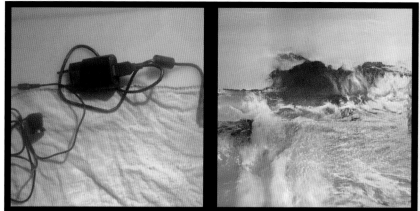

Memo Akten,
Gloomy Sunday,
2017

In this experiment, Akten shows
how a neural network trained
on images of ocean waves, fire,
clouds and flowers will read
them into everything that it sees.

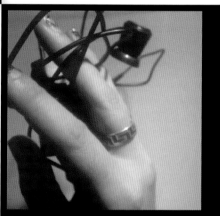

Architectural Hallucinations

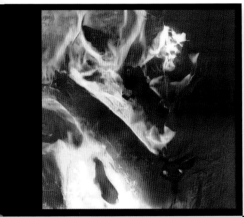

What Can AI Tell Us About the Mind of an Architect?

Can AI help us to understand how the mind works, and how architects think? **Neil Leach**, Professor at Florida International University, points out that, although human intelligence and artificial intelligence are very different things, analogies can be drawn. AI, he argues, can potentially offer us insights into how the mind works, and so too into how architects are trained to think.

Ask any schoolchild how many colours there are in a rainbow. Chances are that they will reply, 'Seven'. In fact there are an infinite number of colours in a rainbow, but schoolchildren are trained to think that there are only seven. Indeed, according to neuroscientist Anil Seth, colour is itself a construct, generated by the brain.[1] Ask any architectural student what a 'functionalist' building looks like. Chances are they will describe a white building on pilotis with a flat roof. In fact flat roofs are hardly functional, as they tend to leak, but architectural students are trained to think that flat roofs are functional. In other words, we see the world not as it is, but as we have been trained to see it.

In this respect we are not dissimilar to neural networks, which also see the world as they have been trained. In *Gloomy Sunday* (2017), computational artist Memo Akten shows how a neural network interprets objects through a particular lens based on its training dataset.[2] If trained on flowers, the neural network will read flowers into everything. As Akten observes, 'The picture we see in our conscious mind is not a mirror image of the outside world, but is a reconstruction based on our expectations and prior beliefs.'[3]

What can AI tell us about the mind of the architect?

Predictive Perception

The theory of predictive perception is now gaining considerable traction. According to Seth, the brain is locked inside the 'boney vault of the skull' without light or sound.[4] The brain therefore attempts its 'best guess' about what is outside, seeking to make sense of a 'constant barrage of electrical signals which are only indirectly related to things out there in the world'.[5] Perception is therefore highly subjective. The brain does not simply receive signals from the outside. It actively partakes in making sense of what it is perceiving: 'Instead of perception depending largely on signals coming into the brain from the outside world, it depends as much, if not more, on perceptual predictions flowing in the opposite direction. We don't just passively perceive the world, we actively generate it. The world we

experience comes as much, if not more, from the inside out as from the outside in.'[6]

Seth argues that the brain therefore makes predictions, on the basis of 'perceptual expectations'.[7] These distort and colour how we see the world. In other words, Akten's notion of perception being based on 'expectations and prior beliefs' is very similar to Seth's notion of it being based on 'perceptual expectations'. In short, there are remarkable parallels between Akten's explorations into human perception using neural networks and Seth's theory of predictive perception.

Seth refers to these predictions as 'hallucinations'. Unlike standard hallucinations, which are uncontrolled and untethered to reality, these hallucinations are controlled to prevent incorrect predictions. This happens through a process of 'prediction error minimisation', a feedback mechanism that registers the difference between what the brain expects and what it actually sees, and updates its perception accordingly, 'reining in' its initial prediction.[8] Thus Seth concludes: 'If hallucination is a kind of controlled perception, then perception right here and right now is also a kind of hallucination, but a controlled hallucination in which the brain's predictions are being reined in by sensory information from the world. In fact, we're all hallucinating all the time, including right now. It's just that when we agree about our hallucinations, we call that reality.'[9]

Can we draw parallels between the 'controlled hallucinations' of the mind and the 'machine hallucinations' of a generative adversarial network (GAN)? Importantly, both involve control. Analogies can be drawn, perhaps, between *uncontrolled* standard hallucinations and the *uncontrolled* hallucinations of DeepDream, and between the *controlled* hallucinations of the mind the *controlled* hallucinations of a GAN. After all, a GAN is based on a competition between one neural network that generates images – a 'generator' – and another – a 'discriminator' – that judges them against a dataset of target images.

Importantly, also, with a neural network there is a corrective process in place, 'backpropagation', that is not

Keisuke Suzuki and Anil Seth, *Hallucination Machine*, 2017

A video processed using a DeepDream algorithm illustrates how overly strong perceptual predictions can lead to weird hallucinatory perceptions, where individuals come to read images of whatever they have been trained on into everything that they see – in this case images of dogs.

dissimilar to the prediction error minimisation of the brain. Backpropagation is a process whereby information about prediction errors propagates backwards through the various layers of the neural network, allowing the original 'weights' to be recalibrated and updated, so that the system can 'converge' or edge closer to the correct answer, in a process not unlike reverse engineering. Resolution is also enhanced by the number of layers – sometimes up to 1,000 – in a neural network and individual training cycles – referred to as 'epochs'.

This process can be understood as a form of 'learning'. AI expert Pedro Domingos observes, 'Learning is what the brain does, and so what we need to do is to reverse engineer it. The brain learns by adjusting the strengths of connections between neurons, and the crucial problem is figuring out which connections are to blame for which errors and changing them accordingly.'[10]

Parallels can therefore be drawn between the prediction error minimisation of the mind and backpropagation of neural networks. AI expert Geoffrey Hinton even speculates that the brain itself undertakes a form of backpropagation.[11]

The 'controlled hallucinations' of the mind and the 'machine hallucinations' of neural networks are in fact not so dissimilar.

The 'controlled hallucinations' of the mind and the 'machine hallucinations' of neural networks are in fact not so dissimilar

Fernando Salcedo,
Architectural Hallucinations,
Master of Architecture,
Florida International University,
Miami,
2020

Salcedo's study used a CycleGAN trained on images of the King Abdullah Petroleum Studies and Research Center in Riyadh, Saudi Arabia, to reinterpret images of clothing on the left in order to produce a hallucination of other possible designs for that building.

Architecturalisations

Could we also compare our training as architects to the training of neural networks? Florida International University (FIU) architecture student Fernando Salcedo conducted an AI experiment, Architectural Hallucinations (2020), similar to *Gloomy Sunday*, training a neural network on a research centre designed by Zaha Hadid Architects (ZHA).[12] The neural network then reads architectural forms into everything it sees, including items of clothing, through a process similar to predictive perception. In this weirdly distorted view, a crumpled T-shirt is read as a warped ZHA project. Importantly, the neural network reads these forms through a filter. This experiment raises some interesting questions. Is this perhaps how architects see the world, reading potential buildings into everything that they see? In other words, does the architectural mind operate a little like a neural network?

To claim that this is the case would be an argument based on pure analogy. Nonetheless it is tempting to pursue this line of enquiry further. Might this experiment offer insights, for example, into the nature of inspiration itself – the act of reading the world through a particular lens and then re-expressing that vision through design? Are we trained to interpret external forms just as a neural network is trained to interpret images? Equally, might we also hallucinate architectural designs based on our training, just like a neural network?

We could describe this process as a form of 'architecturalisation'. In effect architects tend to 'architecturalise' the world and read it in architectural terms. As with DeepDream, they are trained on a specific dataset. They see the world in terms of potential buildings. This allows architects to be inspired by various non-architectural items – such as biological entities and geological formations – and incorporate them into their architectural expressions. This might explain, for example, how Jørn Utzon was inspired by the billowing sails of

Giovanna Pillaca, *Futuristic Temple in India,* 2021

above and opposite: Images generated through CLIP and VQGAN, each of them based on the prompts 'Futuristic Temple in India' and the pre-prompts 'Ma Yansong', 'Morphosis Architects' and 'Wolf Prix'. Traces of the works included in the prompts and pre-prompts are vaguely recognisable in the generated images.

yachts in Sydney Harbour, and read them as potential vaults for the design of his opera house. This principle is not dissimilar to reading faces into clouds, or making sense of Pointillist paintings by 'joining the dots'.

By extension, this would also explain how architects tend to 'aestheticise' the world, reading it in aesthetic terms, and rinsing it of economic, social and political considerations.[13] Why is it, for example, that many architects tend to privilege design concerns over economic concerns, even though economic factors are the driver of any design? Indeed, why are there so few economic references in books on architecture, apart from the cost on their back covers? It is as though architects tend to see the world through a rose-tinted, aestheticising lens.

This tendency becomes even more obvious, however, in reverse – when, instead of interpreting an image, such as reading a face in a cloud, we translate a concept into a visual image. An obvious example of this would be recent images generated using CLIP and VQGAN based on textual prompts. Does this reflect how architects conjure up an initial sketch impression, based on a design brief and the dataset on which they are trained?

This might also help to explain, for example, why architects so often misinterpret philosophical concepts, such as the 'fold' in Gilles Deleuze's writings, as though they refer to architectural forms, when they actually have nothing to do with architecture. Rather, according to philosopher Simon Sullivan, the concept of the fold allows Deleuze to think creatively about the production of human and nonhuman forms of subjectivity.[14] The same happened with Jacques Derrida. Architects seemed to think that 'deconstruction' referred to the construction of buildings, whereas in fact it refers to our 'constructed' understanding of the world, such as believing that flat roofs are functional. As Derrida puts it, there is an 'architecture of architecture'.[15] Our understanding of construction is itself constructed.

It might additionally explain some architects' mistake of assuming terms referring to the digital – such as 'discrete'– refer potentially to architectural forms, even though the digital itself is immaterial and without form.[16] It might equally explain how historians read that Big Data is 'messy', and therefore assume the architectural style of Big Data must also be messy.[17] These misguided attempts to read architectural form into abstract concepts are perfect examples of the problem of 'architecturalisation'.

It is important to understand, then, that the gaze of the architect is not innocent. Architects see the world not as it is, but as they have been trained, and re-create that vision in their designs.

In the Mirror of AI

Let us be clear. The meaning of any term varies according to its context. Machine 'learning' and human 'learning', for example, are quite different, as are artificial 'intelligence' and human 'intelligence'. There is a significant difference between AI and human intelligence, not least because AI does not possess consciousness – at least for now. We must be cautious of projecting human attributes onto AI – and vice versa. Likewise, 'machine hallucinations' and 'human hallucinations' are not the same.

There are moments, however, when neural networks offer insights into human intelligence, and parallels present themselves. Of course, in such instances, parallels remain just parallels. A behaviour in one domain does not explain a similar behaviour in another. But nonetheless, digital simulations can often help us to understand analogue behaviours. For example, it was not until artificial life expert Craig Reynolds simulated the flocking behaviour of birds using 'boids', in 1986, that we could understand the behaviour of actual birds.[18] It is as though AI might help become a mirror in which to understand human intelligence.

Might AI also help us, then, to understand the mind of the architect? ⌂

Notes
1. Anil Seth, *Being You: A New Science of Consciousness*, Dutton (London), 2021, p 115.
2. Memo Akten, 'Learning to See: Gloomy Sunday', Memo.tv, 2017: www.memo.tv/portfolio/gloomy-sunday/.
3. *Ibid*.
4. Seth, *op cit*, p 75.
5. Seth, 'Your Brain Hallucinates Your Conscious Reality', TED Talk, April 2017: www.ted.com/talks/anil_seth_your_brain_hallucinates_your_conscious_reality?language=en.
6. *Ibid*.
7. Seth, *Being You, op cit, passim*.
8. *Ibid*, p 83.
9. Seth, 'Your Brain Hallucinates Your Conscious Reality', *op cit*.
10. Pedro Domingos, *The Master Algorithm: Why the Quest for the Ultimate Learning Machine Will Remake the World*, Basic Books (New York), 2018, p 52.
11. Geoffrey Hinton, 'Can the Brain Do Backpropagation?', Stanford Seminar, 27 April 2018: https://youtu.be/VIRCybGgHts.
12. Fernando Salcedo, 'Deep Perception | M.Arch Thesis', 17 April 2020: https://youtu.be/WCsjbPc9624.
13. See Neil Leach, *The Anaesthetics of Architecture*, MIT Press (Cambridge, MA), 1999.
14. Simon Sullivan, 'The Fold', in Adrian Parr (ed), *The Deleuze Dictionary*, Edinburgh University Press (Edinburgh), 2012, p 107.
15. Neil Leach, *Rethinking Architecture: A Reader in Cultural Theory*, Routledge (London), 1997, p 307.
16. Neil Leach, 'There Is No Such Thing as a Digital Building: A Critique of the Discrete,' in Gilles Retsin (ed), *⌂ Discrete: Reappraising the Digital in Architecture*, March/April (no 2), 2019, p 139.
17. Mario Carpo, *The Second Digital Turn: Design Beyond Intelligence*, MIT Press (Cambridge, MA), 2017.
18. Craig Reynolds, 'Flocks, Herds, and Schools: A Distributed Behavioral Model', *Computer Graphics* 21 (4), 1987, pp 25–34.

AI-CONTROLLED ROBOT MASKS

Behnaz Farahi,
AI-Controlled Robotic Masks,
2020

The masks are intended to empower
women and allow them to communicate
with one another.

Behnaz Farahi

RESISTING
PATRIARCHAL
OPPRESSION

Using computational techniques to foster new empathetic relationships between human bodies and the space around them, **Behnaz Farahi**, Assistant Professor in the Department of Design at the California State University in Long Beach, presents some of the concepts and events that have inspired her research and focuses on a recent project for an interactive niqab.

The Bandari women from the southern coast of Iran are famous for their intriguing niqab masks.[1] Made of various colourful materials, and designed to reflect the status of the wearer, they completely cover the forehead and the nose, with only the wearer's eyes left visible. Legend has it that the practice started during Portuguese colonial rule (1587–1629), as a way of protecting the wearer not only from the harsh sun of the Persian Gulf, but also from slave masters looking for pretty women. From a contemporary perspective, the masks can be seen as a means of protecting women from patriarchal and colonial oppression.

In her seminal article 'Can the Subaltern Speak?' (1988), feminist theorist Gayatri Spivak asks whether it might be possible for the colonised – the subaltern – to have a voice in the face of colonial oppression.[2] How might this same question be reframed in the context of contemporary digital culture? Is there a way for the subaltern to speak that would also undermine the power of the oppressor?

Masking Meaning

A 2017 experiment involving two artificial intelligence bots at Facebook AI Research (FAIR) might give us some insights. The intention was to create chatbots that could negotiate in order to hold meaningful conversations with people. The aim of the researchers was to show that it is possible for agents to engage in a negotiation and come to an agreement, similar to how people might have conflicting goals and negotiate in order to come to an agreement on something.[3] A problem started to manifest itself, however, when the bots started to learn from each other's mistakes, without knowing they were repeating the mistakes. Their conversation started to degenerate and they began to repeat words, giving the impression that they had started to formulate their own language – a language that no human could understand. The researchers decided to intervene and terminate the experiment. Besides the fact that it shows that AI can be used for natural language generation, this story also reveals how the authority of those in power can be undermined by that which they cannot understand. Knowledge is power, and an inability to understand unnerves those who wish to maintain their authority.

Facebook AI Research (FAIR) experiment, 2017

The text generated by two AI bots in the Facebook AI lab when the bots began to communicate with a degenerate form of English after too many rounds of reinforcement learning.

```
Bob: i can i i everything else . . . . . . . . . . . . . . .
Alice: balls have zero to me to me to me to me to me to m
Bob: you i everything else . . . . . . . . . . . . . . .
Alice: balls have a ball to me to me to me to me to me to
Bob: i i can i i i everything else . . . . . . . . . . . .
Alice: balls have a ball to me to me to me to me to me to
Bob: i . . . . . . . . . . . . . . . . . . . . . .
Alice: balls have zero to me to me to me to me to me to m
Bob: you i i i i i everything else . . . . . . . . . . . .
Alice: balls have 0 to me to me to me to me to me to me t
Bob: you i i i everything else . . . . . . . . . . . . . .
Alice: balls have zero to me to me to me to me to me to m
```

Can the subaltern speak?

-.-.. .- -./ - .....- / ... ..- -.... .- --. - .. . -.-.-./ ... .-- . . -. .--. .----..

آیا فرودست می تواند سخن بگوید؟

Behnaz Farahi,
AI-Controlled Robotic Masks,
2020

Can the subaltern speak? A machine-learning
algorithm generates texts and translates them
into eye blinks using Morse Code.

The use of code as a secret message also has an interesting history. As is well known, the Navajo language was used as code during the Second World War,[4] while Alan Turing's use of computation to crack the Nazi Enigma code helped to curtail that war.[5] But there have been other examples since then. In 1966, during an interview by his captors for a propaganda video during the Vietnam War, Admiral Jeremiah Denton secretly delivered the message 'T-O-R-T-U-R-E' in plain sight by blinking it in Morse Code, feigning trouble with his eyes from the bright television lights. More recently still, during the Covid-19 shutdown, women have been using the code word 'Mask 19' to report domestic violence at pharmacies in France, inspired by a similar scheme in Spain.[6]

Mask Design

The AI-Controlled Robotic Masks project is a similar 'experiment' that brings these three examples together – the subversion of the niqab mask, the unsettling behaviour of the AI bots and the use of code to deliver secret messages – to develop a subversive strategy to empower women under patriarchy. Using a Markov chain – a common machine-learning algorithm for statistically modelling random processes – each mask learns and develops a 'language' based on a source text. The first mask starts with an excerpt from Spivak's 'Can the Subaltern Speak?'. It then offers a variation of this based on the probability of the juxtaposition of letters, for example the probability of the letter 'e' appearing after 'th'.

In the fields of computational linguistics and probability, this is known as an 'n-gram', which is 'a contiguous sequence of n items from a given sample of text or speech'.[7] In this case, the n-grams of a given text provide a strategy for generating the next text. The Markov chain could therefore be used to generate a text where each new letter is dependent on the previous letter/s or even

sequence of words. This algorithm could be constructed based on probabilities of a large body of source text or as short as a sentence. As the masks communicate, the algorithm is repeated and the n-gram changes. The smaller the n-grams become, the less linguistic meaning there is in the generated text.

Meanwhile, each mask also receives the biometric information of the wearer by tracking the openness of their eyelid in real time, and records, analyses and learns from the movement of the opposite mask. This information informs the speed of the blinking actuators as well as the number associated with a contiguous sequence of items in a given sample, known as n-grams. Technically speaking, each letter generated through this process is translated into Morse Code, which informs the movement of the actuators; for example, 'H' is 'dot-dot-dot-dot' and 'W' is 'dot-dash-dash'. For this purpose, each mask is equipped with a microcontroller, a small proximity sensor which tracks the movement of the wearer's eyelid, 18 micro-electromagnetic actuators and their driver boards.

Using BLE Protocol
For communication between masks

Custom-made proximity sensor
fpr tracking openness of the wearer's eye

Custom-made PCB Board
for controlling 18 electro-magnetic actuators

Micro controller Feather nRF52

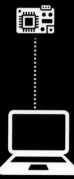

As the masks communicate with each other using the Bluetooth Low Energy (BLE) protocol, the algorithm is repeated and the n-gram for a given sentence changes. The smaller the n-gram becomes, the less linguistic meaning there is in the generated text. After the n-gram reaches 1, the system generates a new sentence and the n-gram returns to 5 again.

Using BLE Protocol
For communication between masks

Custom-made proximity sensor
fpr tracking openness of the wearer's eye

Custom-made PCB Board
for controlling 18 electro-magnetic actuators

Micro controller
Feather nRF52

Each mask receives the biometric information of the wearer by tracking the openness of their eyelid in real time, and records, analyses and learns from the movement of the opposite mask

Apart from being a social and political commentary on ways of subverting patriarchy, the robotic masks could also offer insights into how masks might be an opportunity for communication and social interaction

The video documentation of the project[8] shows two women wearing masks covered with eyelashes controlled by AI. They begin to develop their own language to communicate with each other, blinking their eyelashes in rapid succession, using Morse code and the Bluetooth Low Energy (BLE) protocol. Here the 'wink' of the sexual predator is subverted into a language that protects the female figures from the advances of the predator. The aim is to develop a secret language for transmitting information between multiple women.

Developing a new language is extremely challenging for two main reasons. Firstly, while AI systems such as Siri and IBM's Watson can answer basic questions, they do not have any 'real understanding' of the meaning of the words they use. Secondly, the production of language has a complex set of requirements. As Noah Goodman of Stanford University's Department of Psychology states: 'Language is special in that it relies on a lot of knowledge about language but it also relies on a huge amount of common-sense knowledge about the world, and those two go together in very subtle ways.'[9] Goodman and his team have developed a programming language called Webppl that gives computers a type of probabilistic common-sense rather than literal meaning of a given word. For instance, it can predict whether the sentence 'a client is waiting forever for a table' relies more on the context than the literal meaning of the words. More recently, Generative Pre-trained Transformer 3 (GPT-3), an autoregressive language model that uses deep learning to produce human-like text, has been released by San Francisco-based artificial intelligence research laboratory OpenAI. The results seem to be quite convincing, to the point that in many cases it is difficult to distinguish them from texts written by humans. However, whether GPT-3 is capable of actual 'thinking' is still questionable.

Unmasking Emotions

Apart from being a social and political commentary on ways of subverting patriarchy, the robotic masks described and illustrated here could also offer insights into how masks might be an opportunity for communication and social interaction. In the context of the Covid-19 pandemic, where we have to cover our faces, thereby masking our emotional expressions, it is important to think about how we might be able to express ourselves and communicate more effectively. Such a system might also benefit those who suffer from auditory impairment or hearing loss. ⌂

Each mask consists of a total of 18 micro-electromagnetic actuators with fake eyelashes that give the illusion of 18 blinking eyes looking at the viewer. The actuators are able to rotate around one axis according to the polarity of the electrically controlled magnetic coil.

Notes
1. Rodolfo Contreras, 'The Mysterious Masked Women of Iran', BBC.com, 10 January 2017: www.bbc.com/travel/gallery/20170106-the-mysterious-masked-women-of-iran.
2. Gayatri Chakravorty Spivak, 'Can the Subaltern Speak?', in Cary Nelson (ed), *Marxism and the Interpretation of Culture*, University of Illinois Press (Urbana, IL), reprint edn, 1988, pp 66–111.
3. Mike Lewis *et al*, 'Deal or No Deal? End-to-End Learning for Negotiation Dialogues', arxiv.org, 16 June 2017: https://arxiv.org/pdf/1706.05125.pdf.
4. Zachary Spalding, 'Experiences of the Navajo Code Talkers in World War Two', 19 April 2019: http://hdl.handle.net/2022/22973.
5. Charles Severance, 'Alan Turing and Bletchley Park', *Computer* 45 (6), June 2012, pp 6–8.
6. Ivana Kottasová and Valentina Di Donato, 'Women are Using Code Words at Pharmacies to Escape Domestic Violence During Lockdown', CNN.com, 6 April 2020: www.cnn.com/2020/04/02/europe/domestic-violence-coronavirus-lockdown-intl/index.html.
7. Yun Li *et al*, 'A Query Understanding Framework for Earth Data Discovery', *Applied Science* 10 (3), February 2020, p 26.
8. https://vimeo.com/416233417.
9. Will Knight, 'AI's Language Problem', *MIT Technology Review*, 9 August 2016: www.technologyreview.com/2016/08/09/158125/ais-language-problem/.

M Casey Rehm and Damjan Jovanovic

ASSEMBLED WORLDS

NEW CAMPO MARZIO – PIRANESI IN THE AGE OF AI

lifeforms.io (Damjan Jovanovic and Lidija Kljakovic) and Studio Kinch (M Casey Rehm), New Campo Marzio, 2020

opposite: Two autonomous characters negotiate a hypostyle zone within New Campo Marzio. These regions are defined by dense clusters of columns learned by the neural network predominantly from the southeast portion of Piranesi's 'Ichnographia'.

above: Two autonomous characters near the boundary of New Campo Marzio. The boundary of the simulation is a mirrored wall to imply the unending nature of the simulated world.

New Campo Marzio is a collaboration between **Damjan Jovanovic** and Lidija Kljakovic of lifeforms.io and **M Casey Rehm** of Studio Kinch. Jovanovic and Rehm are also faculty at the Southern California Institute of Architecture (SCI-Arc). They have used AI and game engines to create a new vision for the iconic public space in Rome, inspired by and inputting data from Giovanni Battista Piranesi's seminal architectural plan of it from 1762.

Giovanni Battista Piranesi's *Il Campo Marzio dell'Antica Roma* (1762) is one of the most important and revered architectural documents of all time, and has been the subject of numerous studies, research projects and design (re)imaginings. The central piece of the work is the famous 'Ichnographia' or plan of the Campus Martius in Rome, an intricate foldout etching that has long fascinated and excited architects and scholars. The enduring allure and mystery of this drawing is in its unclear ontological status: is it an attempt at factual archaeological recording, a utopian, radical vision of a future city or something else entirely? Peter Trummer sums up the general sentiment clearly: 'With time, Piranesi's plan of Campo Marzio has become our law, testament, commandment or oracle.'[1]

This sentiment is one of the main reasons for lifeforms.io and Studio Kinch's explorations into transposing the work of Piranesi into a new kind of architectural drawing. New Campo Marzio focuses on exploring the possibilities of AI for form generation and in the application of game-engine technologies for representing the New Campo in real time. The result is a new kind of format for architectural representation – indeed, a new kind of drawing.

New Campo Marzio is a self-playing, open-ended simulation of a world imbued with characters and objects.[2] The world is modelled as a dynamic, AI-generated tableau in which the objects and characters deploy behaviour trees to run decision-making. In this way, it tests the boundaries of storytelling and meaning-making by creating a nonlinear, unpredictable narrative structure of a model world from within.

The City and its Characters

At the core of New Campo Marzio is the dynamic relationship between two kinds of AI entities: the AI-generated City, which is made in real time by learning the features of Piranesi's original drawing, and a host of agents that use the behaviour tree logic to navigate, explore and interact with the ever-new Campo versions.

The City is visible as a three-dimensional point cloud and governs its relationships to the user characters through an invisible navigation field composed of colliders, walkable surfaces and procedurally evolving destinations. It is generated through both artificial neural networks (ANNs) and symbolic intelligent agents. These two forms of narrow intelligence require fundamentally different approaches to authorship by the designer.

A generative adversarial network (GAN), the ANN is a predictive intelligence which produces its output through assembled, learned probabilities. When working with this type of intelligence the designer frames intention through the curation of training materials. The ambiguous ontology of Piranesi's *Campo Marzio* makes it an excellent candidate for the reconstruction of its sampled information into new readings. Additionally, the heterogeneity of represented architectural and urban features in the drawing allows for dramatically different interpretations depending on the resolution and framing of the samples taken. Michael Young frames the plan as an 'entourage of objects', a reading

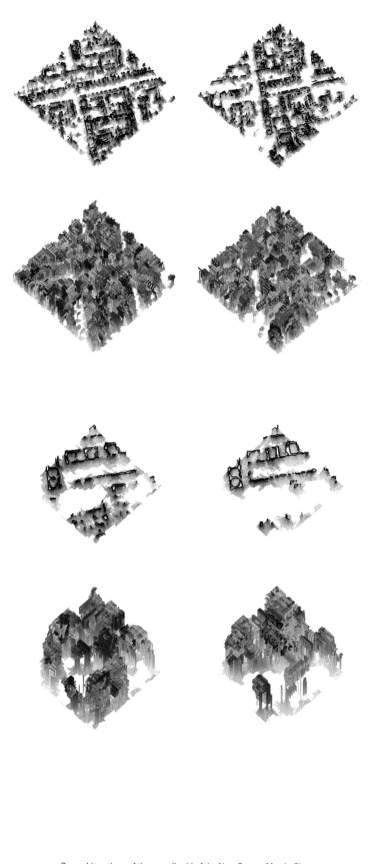

Several iterations of the overall grid of the New Campo Marzio City and smaller cropped locations with sectional cuts show the features learned from Piranesi's *Campo Marzio* plan drawing, while the clouds reveal the transformation of the map into three-dimensional figures through intelligent agent algorithms. A new map is generated by the simulation every five minutes with near-infinite variations.

supported by lower-resolution reproductions of the drawing that show the features in solid black.[3] The original etchings, when viewed in detail, suggest a more continuous reading where architectural elements emerge from the ground through the density of hatches.

In New Campo Marzio, the City's neural network is trained on samples with resolutions between these two extremes. The utilised regions of the plan are at a scale where the larger figures of the drawing are not yet legible, but the resolution of the etchings becomes solid. The dataset's resolution was iterated through engagement with the user characters to emphasise their negotiation with a multitude of architectural conditions, including hypostyle halls, colonnades, cell-like rooms, alleys and plazas, all of which are embedded within Piranesi's original etchings.

A directed latent walk, based on the current positions of the digital occupants, produces a new map from this neural network every five minutes. The map is a probability grid determining solid-void relationships of the City, and symbolic intelligent agents then translate these probabilities into the final point clouds and navigation paths. The neural network governs the overall distribution and composition of material in the scene, taking advantage of its ability to learn hierarchical relationships from its dataset. The symbolic intelligent agents allow a more direct resolution of specific details in the final model.

The characters in New Campo Marzio are procedurally generated robot creatures inspired equally by John Hejduk's 1984 competition entry for a memorial park, *Victims*, and Japanese anime such as *Ghost in the Shell*.[4] Every character has a unique moveset as a way of navigating the City, and a unique animated response to different states triggered by outside stimuli. The characters are a stand-in for the player, and serve to orient the viewer and focus their attention on the simulation.

Three characters are shown in an alley-like section of the generated City. These spaces are defined by linear voids bound on either side by dense point-cloud masses. The brightly coloured masses within the point cloud are sampled from 3D scans of flower arrangements.

New Rules of Engagement

Real-time simulations are an emerging format for architectural representation. Going beyond drawing, mapping and diagramming, they allow for the coexistence of continuous scales within the same model space, and dynamic, real-time interaction with the viewer, potentially raising novel questions about the nature of models and modelling in the disciplinary sense.

In contemporary culture, simulations are present mostly through the medium of video games, which are defined by their ability to offer an interactive, playable, immersive experience of a fully modelled virtual space at any scale – from the apartment block of *The Sims* to the entire universes in games like *No Man's Sky* or *Stellaris*. At the same time, the work of the artist Ian Cheng explores the concept of 'worlding', which he defines as 'the unnatural art of creating an infinite game by choosing a present, storytelling its past, simulating its futures, and nurturing its changes'.[5] The concept of an 'infinite game' comes from James P Carse,[6] and offers a window into some of the ideological motivations behind the work. Working with simulations privileges open-ended structure and presupposes a non-deterministic universe as a liberation from fixed and finite models of thinking and making.

Working with simulations privileges open-ended structure and presupposes a non-deterministic universe

The cell-like regions of the City feature more wall-like enclosures and terraced floor slabs which the characters navigate vertically.

Open plazas emerge within the City. Like those in Piranesi's original drawings, they are defined less by a figural plan and more as the result of voids within the dense assembly of material.

In many ways, the idea represents a narrative paradigm that hybridises cinema (animation) and games, where the traditional narrative structures are placed in friction and in an adversarial relationship with the open-endedness and chaotic beauty of a simulation. The classical tropes of storytelling that have always governed how we understand and assign meaning are incapable of regulating the chaos of a simulation, thus breaking our own attentional structure and inviting us to develop new rules of engagement.

The notion of montage, understood as the bringing together of parts of separate and distinct worlds into the same frame of vision, is completely absent in a simulation and replaced with the continuous movement of a dynamic camera within the frame. This is a fundamentally different, software-based way of seeing that is only possible in a video game, or through the format of a simulation.

New Campo Marzio uses this logic to drive the automated camera scripts that enable the viewer to immerse themselves in the world through a kind of fluid, continuous, no-cut gaze. There is no 'neutral' camera view in the work – every view frames and follows a character for a limited time before jumping off to a randomly chosen next one in a continuous automated dance. The project operates within the cultural space of the simulation, and explores the significance of this format for architectural design. A fully automated visual work, it is non-deterministic and unique in every iteration of its performance. ⌀

Notes
1. Peter Trummer, 'Introduction', *SAC Journal 5 – Zero Piranesi*, 2020, p 6.
2. https://www.youtube.com/watch?v=4LOT_wzuNoU.
3. Michael Young, 'The Paradigm of Piranesi's Campo Marzio Ichnographia', *SAC Journal 5 – Zero Piranesi*, 2020, p 56.
4. *Ghost in the Shell* (1995), directed by Mamoru Oshii, produced by Production IG.
5. Ian Cheng, *Emissaries Guide to Worlding*, Koenig Books (London), 2018, p 7.
6. James P Carse, *Finite and Infinite Games*, Free Press (New York), 2013.

Immanuel Koh,
3D-GAN-Housing,
'Neural Sampling' series,
Artificial-Architecture research group,
Singapore University of Technology and Design (SUTD),
Singapore, 2021

By deliberately training a 'not-too-perfect' and 'fallible' GAN deep neural network model, high-rise housing forms emerge as indeterminant configurations, traversing the 'uncanny ridge' of habitable/buildable and unhabitable/unbuildable architecture.

Immanuel Koh

ARCHITECTURAL PLASTICITY

THE AESTHETICS OF NEURAL SAMPLING

Director of Artificial-Architecture at the Singapore University of Technology and Design (SUTD), Hokkien Foundation Career Professorship recipient **Immanuel Koh** enlightens us on the wonderful world of deep neural networks, formal plasticity and what they could mean for architectural form-finding.

What is 'architectural plasticity'? A plasticity *in vivo*, *in silico* or *in situ*? In her 2008 book *What Should We Do with Our Brain?*, French philosopher Catherine Malabou writes that 'the word *plasticity* has two basic senses: it can mean the capacity to *receive* form (clay is called "plastic," for example) and the capacity to *give* form (as in the plastic arts or in plastic surgery).'[1] She then adds a third sense – the 'explosion' of form (as with reference to the French words *plastiquage* and *plastiquer*), which she calls 'destructive plasticity', such as in the neurodegenerative disorder of Alzheimer's disease. However, it is only more than a decade later with the publication of her book *Morphing Intelligence: From IQ Measurement to Artificial Brains* (2021) that she begins to assert this same 'plasticity' as the key in establishing a 'mirroring' relationship between the brain and the computer. This reconciliation of the seemingly opposing notion of brain plasticity with that of machine automaticity would in turn inscribe 'within the machine a fallibility that alone makes it intelligent'.[2] To Professor of Rhetoric David Bates, this 'fallibility' is a challenge; as he puts it in his text 'Automaticity, Plasticity, and the Deviant Origins of Artificial Intelligence' (2015), 'the challenge of creating any intelligent automata is the challenge of modeling indetermination, disruption, failure, and error.'[3]

Dreaming Neural Plasticity

Deep neural networks (DNNs) in contemporary AI are machines of automaticity that imitate brain plasticity. They are therefore able to 'receive', 'give' and 'explode' form, yet are also inscribed with a conceptually similar 'fallibility' for their capacity to generate forms. Just as no two human brains conceive of form identically, so too no two DNNs give or train form exactly, even if they share a relatively similar 'received' form, anatomically at birth as in the brain, or architecturally at initialisation as in the machine. Malabou's 'exploding' form even found its expression in the failure modes of deep generative neural networks such as the 'mode collapse' in general adversarial networks (GANs) and the 'exploding gradients' in recurrent neural networks (RNNs). Mode collapse happens when the network over-optimises while being trapped in a local minimum, thus failing to generate a diversity of output samples – a stably overfitting convergence. Conversely, exploding gradient happens when the network experiences drastic and erroneous fluctuations in its weights, thus failing to learn – an unstably underfitting divergence. In simpler terms, overfitting and underfitting are the inabilities to generalise from the input training dataset.

Immanuel Koh,
3D-GAN-Ar-Chair-tecture,
'Neural Sampling' series,
Artificial-Architecture research group,
Singapore University of Technology and Design (SUTD),
Singapore,
2020

Deep neural networks in contemporary AI are machines of automaticity that imitate brain plasticity. They are therefore able to 'receive', 'give' and 'explode' form, yet are also inscribed with a conceptually similar 'fallibility' for their capacity to generate forms

An array of 3D prints sampled from the 'chair-building' latent space showing the ontological irreverence and scalar indifference of the smooth interpolation between 'chair-ness' and 'building-ness'. Recognisable silhouettes of a side chair (leftmost) and a slab block building (rightmost) can be readily observed, alongside hybrid ones with unusual structural connectivity.

The 3D print of an output sampled from the GAN's 'chair' latent space exhibits an uncanny 'chair-ness' that is derived from several chair types found in the training set, such as side chairs, armchairs, club chairs, swivel chairs, folding chairs and cantilever chairs. Multi-axial asymmetries, unexpected discontinuities and contradictory fragmentations can be readily observed, such as at the backrest, armrest, legs, base and seat.

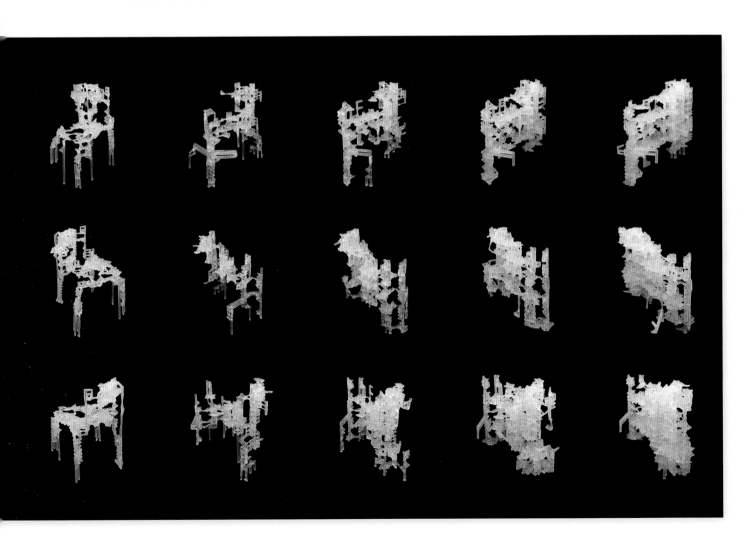

In his 2021 paper 'The Overfitted Brain: Dreams Evolved to Assist Generalization', neuroscientist and neurophilosopher Erik Hoel proposes the radical 'overfitted brain hypothesis' (OBH), which states that the overfitting of artificial neural networks (ANNs) is often avoided by 'sampling from an out-of-distribution' dataset during training; and in a similar vein, the human brain avoids overfitting 'by hallucinating out-of-distribution sensory stimulation every night' during dreaming.[4] In other words, the sampling of fallibility (noisy and corrupted inputs) is a precondition for intelligence.

In a 2020 post on his 'Dreaming and Sampling' blog, Adobe research scientist Aaron Hertzmann alludes to a similar hypothesis with the 'wake-sleep algorithm' proposed by AI pioneer Geoff Hinton in the 1990s.[5] Hertzmann is also the author of two papers: 'Aesthetics of Neural Network Art' (2019) and 'Visual Indeterminacy in GAN Art' (2020). In the former he attempts to establish that neural aesthetics in art are characterised by 'interestingness' (a term borrowed from AI artist Mario Klingemann) which is often the result of the 'unusual juxtapositions of realistic visual cues'.[6] In the latter he proposes the 'uncanny ridge' which is a simple bell curve with 'visual indeterminacy' (another term borrowed, from artist Robert Pepperell) increasing along the y-axis and the 'quality' of generative models improving along the x-axis.[7] It is an illustration that 'powerful-but-imperfect' GANs excel in generating visual indeterminacy or interestingness. However, once the GANs surpass this uncanny ridge and arrive at near-perfect automaticity in producing ordinary imagery, it will be necessary for artists to 'break' the GANs in order to regain indeterminacy. It is at this juncture that we begin to see where artists and architects diverge from computer scientists in their creative search for a plastic ontology with DNNs.

The chair's plasticity does not lie in a latent space, but in a probabilistic sequence, much like language

Immanuel Koh,
3D-Autoregressive-Chair,
'Neural Sampling' series,
Artificial-Architecture research group,
Singapore University of
Technology and Design (SUTD),
Singapore,
2021

The polygonal and faceted formal expression is a result of the neural sampling process which learns and infers from the sequential order of vertices and faces making up the digital 3D geometries from the furniture training set. Destructive plasticity ('exploding forms') can be observed in the familiar yet degenerated and dysfunctional chair and table output samples inferred by the transformer-based autoregressive deep neural network model.

Sampling Architectural Plasticity

One of six modes of architectural sampling, the 'Neural Sampling' series, first introduced as part of a doctoral dissertation at École Polytechnique Fédérale de Lausanne (EPFL)[8] and later extended as part of the Artificial-Architecture research group at the Singapore University of Technology and Design (SUTD), is an attempt to address the specific hierarchical structure of DNNs for architectural design beyond its two-dimensional representations. More recent projects in the same series have successfully operated in three dimensions in articulating the constituents of an architectural plasticity. The 3D-GAN-Ar-chair-tecture was first featured on the online AI Art Gallery of the NeurIPS Workshop on Machine Learning for Creativity and Design 2020, and is a demonstration of 'form sampling' from three 3D-GAN latent spaces trained on thousands of 3D geometric models of chairs and buildings at different scales and resolutions. It is also a counterpoint to the dominant 'form finding' approach of topological optimisation that seeks to arrive at a structural and material ideal via physics-based and constraint-based simulations. Forms are thus granted the plasticity to dream without overfitting to automaticity and without being constrained to explicit multi-objectives.

This ontological plasticity is the underlying interestingness mechanism for interpolating different forms of 'chair-ness' and 'building-ness', yet without the photographic realism that Hertzmann would have insisted on. Neural sampling in this 3D-GAN proceeds by indirectly sampling from a continuous abstract space prior to generating a full 3D form in a 'sampling-all-at-once' process. The 3D-Autoregressive-Chair project (2021), however, is a 'sampling-one-by-one' process and is based on a transformer deep learning model. Neural sampling here proceeds by directly sampling from the discrete 3D vertices and faces of its training dataset – a slow, generative process that samples sequentially, one vertex after another, and then one face after another. Its plasticity does not therefore lie in a latent space, but in a probabilistic sequence, much like in language.

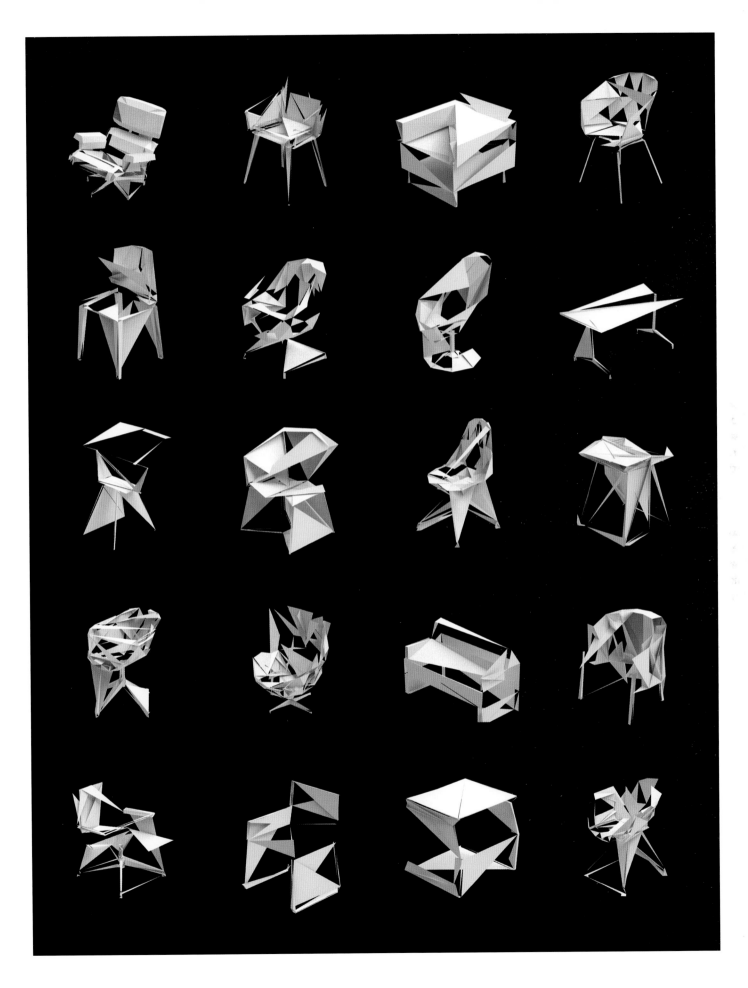

Immanuel Koh,
3D-GAN-Housing,
'Neural Sampling' series,
Artificial-Architecture
research group,
Singapore University of
Technology and Design (SUTD),
Singapore,
2021

right: The 3D-GAN deep neural network struggled during the initial training process (top left to bottom right), but eventually learnt to generate increasingly plausible 3D configurations of high-rise buildings. From the random approximations of building massing blobs of undifferentiated semantics, it eventually learnt to interconnect apartments with communal spaces and circulation cores.

below: A GAN latent walk (top left to bottom right) showing the smooth interpolation of sampled high-rise housing forms whose 'housing-ness' is derived solely from the synthesis of features discovered in its training dataset. These generated hybrid housing forms could be intuitively observed as belonging to a remix of different housing typologies, such as point blocks, slab blocks and cluster blocks.

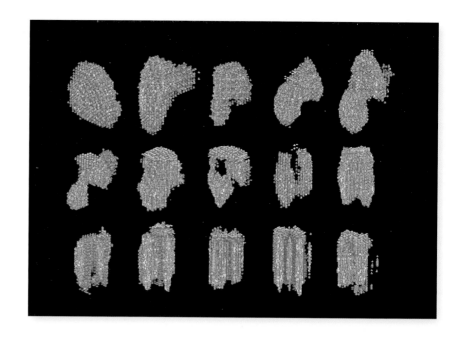

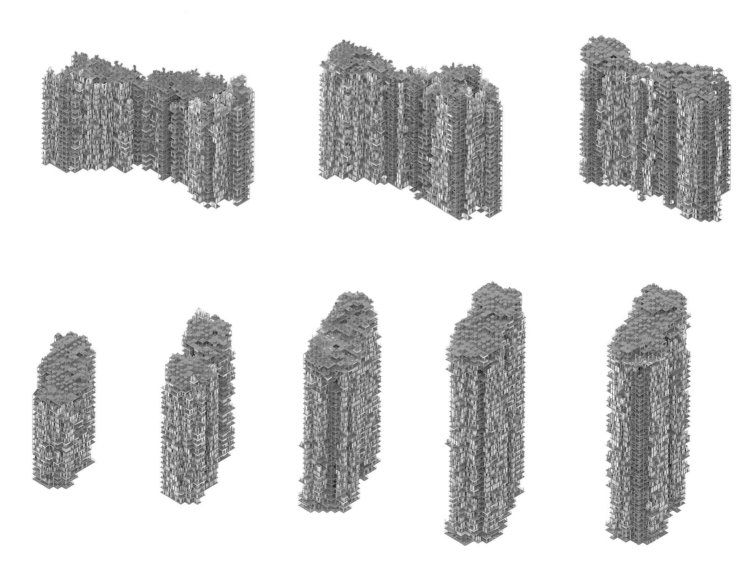

Unlike these projects of formal exteriority, 3D-GAN-Housing, exhibited at the Venice Architecture Biennale in 2021, signals a shift towards incorporating more complex architectural notions of spatial interiority, programmatic semantics and contextual bias with greater granularity. A custom-designed 3D-GAN is trained on thousands of 3D geometric models of Singapore's high-rise public housing flats such that semantically and configurationally plausible housing forms could be sampled from its latent space. Multiple GANs of the same network architecture have been trained and 'broken' differently to explore the so-called 'uncanny ridge', where models are seen yielding a range of formal, spatial and semantic realism suggestive of the inhabitable.

Towards an Architectural Plasticity

De Stijl architect Theo van Doesburg, in his seminal text *'Towards a Plastic Architecture'*, may have been right in envisioning formal plasticity through a reductionism of forms.[9] Postmodern architects, such as Charles Moore, Terry Farrell and John Outram, may have been right in seeking formal diversity through a sampling of histories. A century after the former and half a century after the latter, however, formal reductionism and diversity have instead come to reside in the deep neural network itself – on the one hand by training its neurons and connectivity in plasticity, and on the other by sampling its latent space and probabilistic sequence in generativity. ⌂

Notes
1. Catherine Malabou, *What Should We Do with Our Brain?*, Fordham University Press (New York), 2008, p 5.
2. Catherine Malabou, *Morphing Intelligence: From IQ Measurement to Artificial Brains*, Columbia University Press (New York), 2021, pp 113–14.
3. David Bates, 'Automaticity, Plasticity, and the Deviant Origins of Artificial Intelligence', in David Bates and Nima Bassiri (eds), *Plasticity and Pathology: On the Formation of the Neural Subject*, Fordham University Press (New York), 2015, p 214.
4. Erik Hoel, 'The Overfitted Brain: Dreams Evolved to Assist Generalization', *Patterns* 2 (5), 2021, p 1.
5. 'Dreaming and Sampling': https://aaronhertzmann.com/2020/09/23/dreaming-and-Sampling.html .
6. Aaron Hertzmann, 'Aesthetics of Neural Network Art', arxiv.org, 2019: https://arxiv.org/pdf/1903.05696.pdf.
7. Aaron Hertzmann, 'Visual Indeterminacy in GAN Art', *Leonardo* 53, 2020, pp 424–8.
8. Immanuel Koh, 'Architectural Sampling: A Formal Basis for Machine-Learnable Architecture', PhD thesis, École Polytechnique Fédérale de Lausanne, Switzerland, 2019: http://dx.doi.org/10.5075/epfl-thesis-7815.
9. Theo van Doesburg, 'Towards a Plastic Architecture', 1924. Originally published in *De Stijl*, XII, 6/7, Rotterdam 1924.

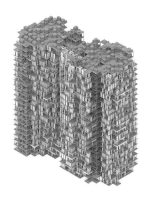

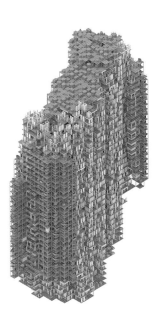
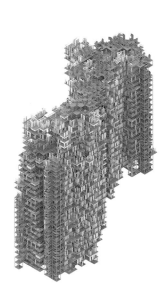
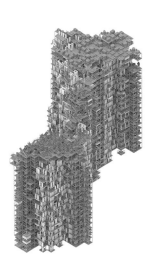

Achim Menges and Thomas Wortmann

Synthesising Artificial Intelligence and Physical Performance

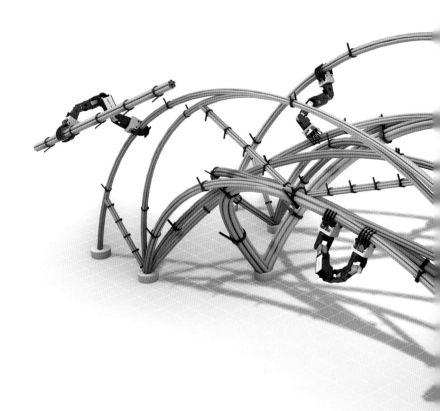

Grzegorz Lochnicki and Nicolas Kubail Kalousdian,
Co-Designing Material-Robot Behaviours:
Systems for Autonomous Construction,
Integrative Technologies and Architectural
Design Research (ITECH) thesis project,
University of Stuttgart,
2020

Trained in a simulated environment, design/builder agents learn to collaboratively bend bamboo culms into a desired shape by using only their body weight and momentum. Based on material feedback, this approach promises new applications in construction for heterogeneous materials that have hitherto been underutilised.

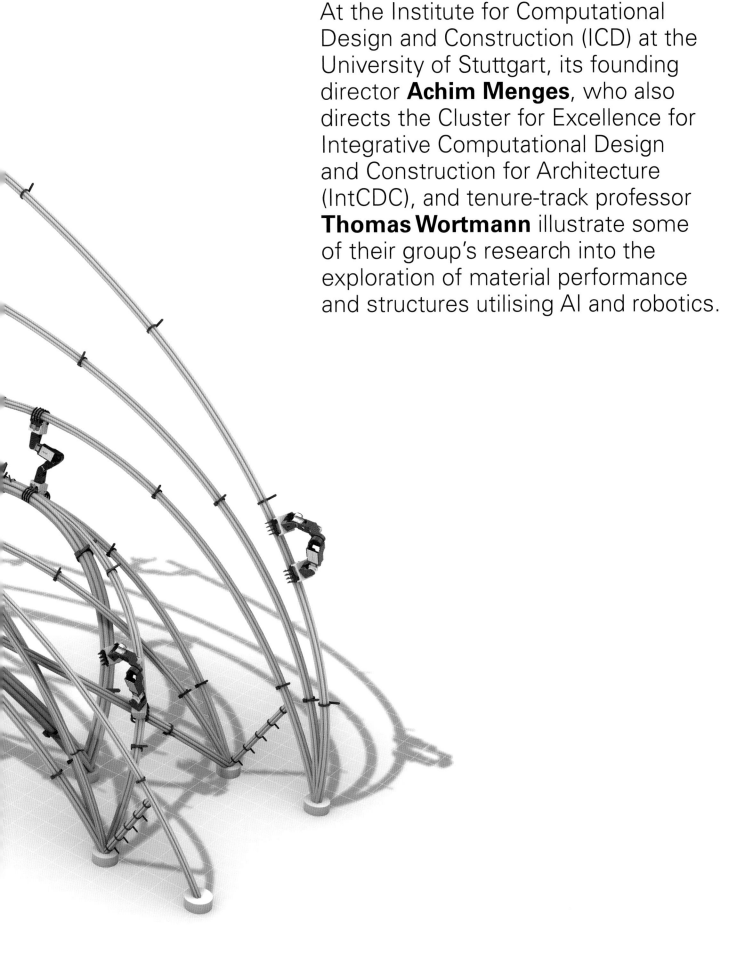

At the Institute for Computational Design and Construction (ICD) at the University of Stuttgart, its founding director **Achim Menges**, who also directs the Cluster for Excellence for Integrative Computational Design and Construction for Architecture (IntCDC), and tenure-track professor **Thomas Wortmann** illustrate some of their group's research into the exploration of material performance and structures utilising AI and robotics.

In architectural practice and academic discourse there is a well-established understanding and shared appreciation of the social and cultural importance of buildings. In recent years, mainly because the detrimental environmental impact of established design and construction approaches[1] has become ever more apparent and can no longer be ignored by the discipline, the ecological facet of architecture is increasingly considered to be deeply interrelated with its cultural dimension. Resource effectiveness and performance, once considered primarily engineering and economic concerns, are progressively repositioned as integral and indispensable drivers for the urgently required rethinking of the intellectual and physical production of architecture – that is, of design and construction.

Performance, as it relates to both the physical structures of buildings and the physical processes of their construction, has been the focus of research at the University of Stuttgart's Institute for Computational Design and Construction (ICD) for many years.[2] While digital technologies are key drivers of this research, it constitutes not only a technical venture, but also an intellectual endeavour to explore an alternative material culture for architecture.[3] One key challenge for a performance-oriented, integrative and interdisciplinary approach is the interaction between computational processes and human design intent, intuition and competence. To enable direct designer interaction, continuous feedback and adaptivity, an agent-based design framework[4] has been developed that combines bottom-up, rule-based, performance-driven modelling methods to handle the complex interrelations and reciprocities of multifaceted performance criteria, with the possibility of directly steering design exploration.

Virtual Design/Builder Agents for Complex Building Systems

In the context of the recently established Cluster of Excellence on Integrative Computational Design and Construction for Architecture (IntCDC) at the University of Stuttgart and the Max Planck Institute for Intelligent Systems,[5] AI methods have become an integral part of the development of this agent-based design framework. They allow going beyond predetermined, hard-coded and fixed behavioural rules towards self-learning, intelligent agent behaviours. This significantly broadens the scope of possible applications, ranging from intelligent virtual agents for designing with complex building systems that gain performance through material differentiation across several scales, to cyber-physical agents for the design of novel construction processes employing distributed robotics as well as the heterogeneous properties of natural materials.

Fibre structures, such as the livMatS Pavilion by the IntCDC and the Integrative Technologies and Architectural Design Research (ITECH) programme, are high-performance building systems which, due to their multiscalar material differentiation, exhibit exceptional structural and material performance. But designing fibre structures is challenging: the location, orientation and density of thousands of fibres needs to be finely calibrated and their material behaviour during production integrated from the start.[6] Fibre components are produced sequentially, by winding a fibre between anchor points to gradually layer and form-find a fibre network. This continuous winding path needs to integrate aesthetic, material and structural requirements. The final form emerges only at the very end of production, as the equilibrium state between all interacting fibres.

Cluster of Excellence IntCDC and Integrative Technologies and Architectural Design Research (ITECH) programme / University of Stuttgart, livMatS Pavilion, Freiburg Botanical Garden, Germany, 2021

Fibrous systems, such as the load-bearing structure of this pavilion made entirely from natural flax fibres, exhibit high structural and material performance. The related challenge of designing the location, orientation and density of thousands of fibres can be addressed by employing AI methods.

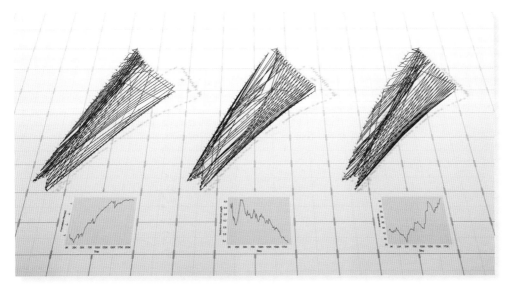

Cluster of Excellence IntCDC/
University of Stuttgart,
Computational Design for Fibre
Composite Building Systems,
2019-22

Reinforcement learning is employed to address
the design challenge of complex fibrous
building systems. The figure shows fibre agents
exploring and learning to construct a fibre net
in three parallel training environments.

The Computational Design for Fibre Composite Building Systems project by the IntCDC's ICD, Visualization Research Center and Machine Learning and Robotics Lab addresses this design challenge by employing reinforcement learning, an AI method where virtual agents are trained in an environment that rewards adaptive behaviours. In the context of robotic construction, reinforcement learning enables a shift from automated towards autonomous or self-governing robotic agents. To find an optimal winding path, a virtual design/builder agent is trained in a simulated environment that rewards goals such as the amount of fibre-to-fibre interaction, segment lengths and fibre directions. In contrast with more traditional optimisation methods, this virtual builder agent can work well on a wide variety of fibre components and thus opens up the possibility of broadening the spectrum of fibre systems in architecture.

Physical Design/Builder Agents for Distributed Robotic Construction

Agent models also challenge established construction with more agile cyber-physical processes. Building construction typically requires fixed-position heavy lifting machines that constrain construction processes to be sequential, since the number of such machines is typically limited. Distributed cyber-physical systems, on the other hand, allow highly parallel, flexible and adaptive construction processes. Recent investigations of distributed robots demonstrate machines that go beyond self-prediction and self-correction to further self-configure and self-organise.[7]

In the Robotic Kinematic System for Parallel Construction project by IntCDC's Physical Intelligence Department at the Max Planck Institute, the ICD and the Machine Learning and Robotics Lab at the University of Stuttgart, a fleet of small, simple and cheap robots is employed to leverage the building material itself in kinematic chains that allow highly parallel construction

processes. AI is used to coordinate this distributed fleet of robots, both in terms of optimising motion planning and adapting the design to the inevitably appearing tolerances and deviations. The robots are therefore design/builder agents in that they adapt their actions to both current conditions and other agents. More self-aware, learning agents allow the transition from a process where distributed robots materialise a design as faithfully as possible under top-down control, to a more flexible process where the design and materialisation emerge together from a bottom-up, self-organising process driven by material feedback. This opens up the possibility of building without blueprint, guided primarily by quantitative and qualitative performance criteria, which profoundly challenges not only our current understanding of design and related methods, but also the socioeconomic framework for the delivery of buildings.

Physical Design/Builder Agents for Building with Natural Heterogeneous Materials

Enabling material feedback is especially critical when employing materials with biological variability and related heterogeneous properties. Extending distributed construction robotics towards building with natural materials is a key aspect of more resource-effective and sustainable architecture. For example, bamboo is a structurally efficient, rapidly renewable plant with a much shorter crop cycle than wood, but is underutilised as a building material due to its geometric and material variation.

For their University of Stuttgart ITECH thesis project Co-Designing Material-Robot Behaviours: Systems for Autonomous Construction, Grzegorz Lochnicki and Nicolas Kubail Kalousdian developed a mobile robotic system and corresponding reinforcement learning approach for climbing on and assembly of bamboo structures. In order to bend and connect bamboo culm bundles, the robots trigger swinging motions of building elements with variable elasticity. The design/builder agents learn, in a simulated environment, to manipulate the radius of elastically bent bamboo culms with their weight, movement and momentum to achieve a desired shape while climbing on unstable and only partially observable structures. In other words, the robots gain self-awareness of their bodies and intuition about the bamboo's material properties, and use this awareness and intuition to interact with individual bamboo culm bundles. In simulated and real-world experiments, this allows the intelligent assembly of active-bending bamboo structures for a wide variety of geometries and material properties. Instead of regarding the biological variation of natural materials as an obstacle, this project leverages it with distributed robotics and AI into an effective, sustainable, light-touch construction method.

Cluster of Excellence IntCDC/
University of Stuttgart
and Max Planck Institute
for Intelligent Systems,
Robotic Kinematic System
for Parallel Construction,
2019-22

A fleet of small, simple and cheap robots allow highly parallel construction processes. AI is used to coordinate the distributed robotic system, both in terms of optimising motion planning and adapting the design on the fly.

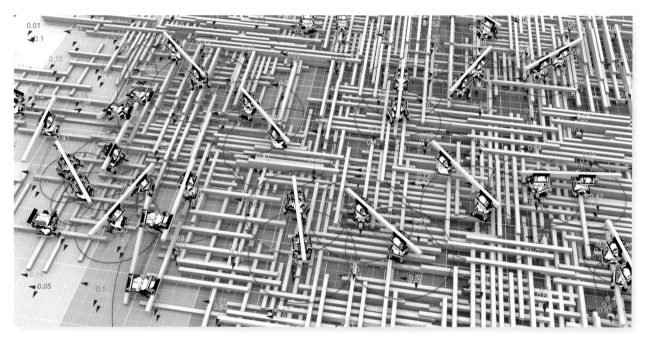

Two physical design/builder agents from a larger fleet of distributed robots walk along a structure, pass each other building elements, and move each other with those elements. In this way, the building elements form part of the kinematic chains for parallel construction.

98

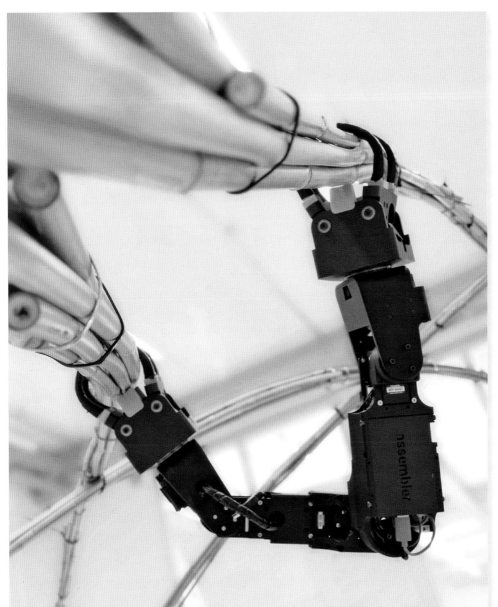

Grzegorz Lochnicki and
Nicolas Kubail Kalousdian,
Co-Designing Material–Robot
Behaviours: Systems for
Autonomous Construction,
Integrative Technologies and
Architectural Design Research
(ITECH) thesis project,
University of Stuttgart,
2020

A mobile robotic system and corresponding reinforcement learning are capable of adapting to variable natural material properties and thus enable the climbing on and assembly of bamboo structures.

Towards a Novel Material Culture in Architecture

Synthesising AI and physical performance in design and construction enables new forms of interaction and collaboration between human designers and virtual as well as physical design and builder agents in order to explore and cultivate alternative, future-proof architectural approaches that are more in tune with the contemporary condition of ecological and social crises and the rapidly growing capabilities of digital technologies. In this way, this synthesis constitutes a crucial facet for the development of novel, urgently required material cultures in architecture.

Trained in a simulated environment, design/builder agents learn to collaboratively bend bamboo culms into a desired shape by using only their body weight and momentum. Based on material feedback, this approach promises new applications in construction for heterogeneous materials that have hitherto been underutilised. ◺

Notes
1. The UN's '2019 Global Status Report for Buildings and Construction Sector' states that the buildings and construction sector accounts for 36 per cent of final energy use and 39 per cent of energy and process-related carbon dioxide (CO_2) emissions, 11 per cent of which resulted from manufacturing building materials: www.unep.org/resources/publication/2019-global-status-report-buildings-and-construction-sector.
2. Achim Menges and Jan Knippers, *Architecture Research Building: ICD/ITKE 2010–2020*, Birkhäuser (Basel), 2021.
3. Achim Menges, ◹ *Computational Material Culture*, March/April (No 2), 2016, pp 76–83.
4. Abel Groenewolt et al, 'An Interactive Agent-based Framework for Materialization-Informed Architectural Design', *Swarm Intelligence* 12 (2), Special Issue on Self-Organised Construction, 2018, pp 155–86.
5. Supported by the German Research Foundation (DFG) under Germany's Excellence Strategy (EXC 2120/1 - 390831618).
6. Achim Menges and Jan Knippers, 'Fibrous Tectonics', in Achim Menges, ◹ *Material Synthesis: Fusing the Physical and the Computational*, September/October (No 5), 2015, pp 40–7.
7. Kirstin H Petersen et al, 'A Review of Collective Robotic Construction', *Science Robotics* 4 (28), 2019.

Text © 2022 John Wiley & Sons Ltd. Images: pp 94–5, 99 Grzegorz Lochnicki / Nicolas Kubail Kalousdian © ITECH / ICD, University of Stuttgart; p 96 Rob Faulkner © ICD / ITKE University of Stuttgart; p 97 Fabian Kannenberg © IntCDC / ICD University of Stuttgart; p 98 Samuel Leder © IntCDC / ICD, University of Stuttgart

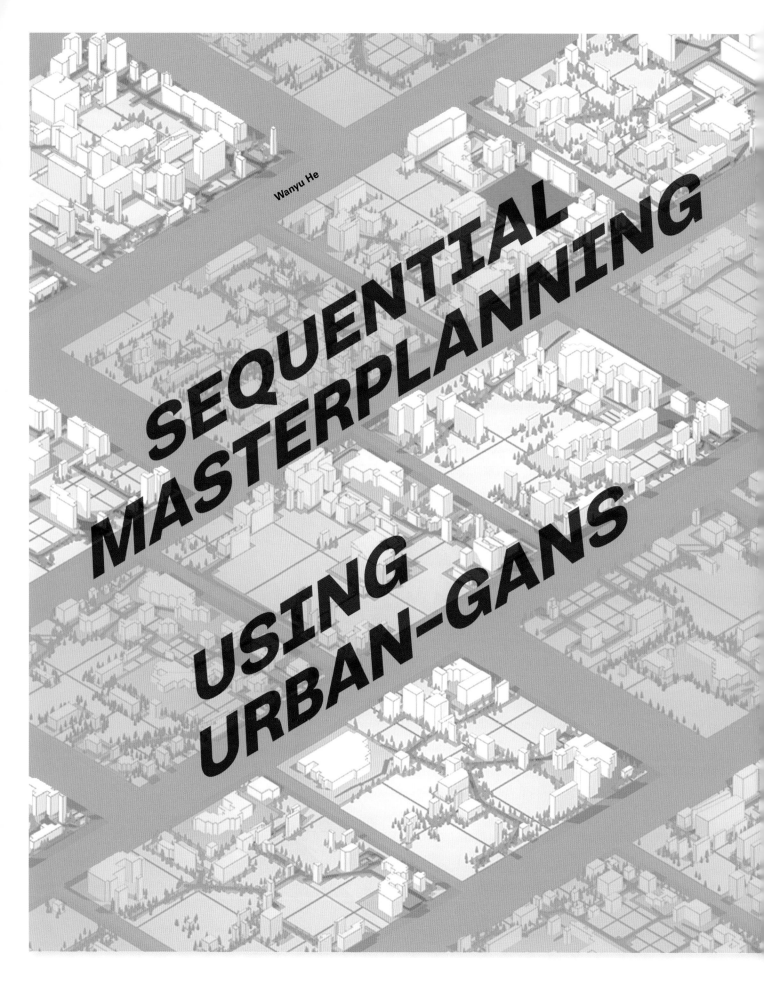

Wanyu He

SEQUENTIAL MASTERPLANNING USING URBAN-GANS

AI, and particularly the use of generative adversarial networks (GANs), can provide a more dynamic urban-planning visual tool allowing the development potential of specific sites to be explored. **Wanyu He** – founder and CEO of XKool Technology, co-founder of Future Architecture Lab and University of Hong Kong academic – explains how.

XKool Technology, Sequential Masterplanning Studies, 2021

The series of 3D masterplanning studies covers a range of periods, with the brighter ones representing the earlier periods.

Generally speaking, urban planning is carried out for a specific moment (usually expressed as the final result), but the dynamic process of its development is rarely observed and studied. The concept of 'time series' attempts to use AI to generate a masterplanning model to show the continuous development of any plot of land over a period of time.

A generative adversarial network (GAN) is used to train this sequential generative planning model to produce a two-dimensional masterplan in several stages. The output of the two-dimensional masterplans will be further represented in 3D to make them easier to understand. The generative model can help any interested party, especially the general public, to see the potential development of any site.

GANs in Urban Planning

Urban or town planning is an activity usually undertaken by professional planners or designers who are responsible for solving the complex problems, and proposing the planning and design solutions that usually determine the fate of a particular site. To achieve 'good' city (or town) planning, planners often find it difficult to measure or control the results with any degree of accuracy, but they can predict the potential of any plot of land in terms of the economy, population, natural environment and other factors. In 1978, Michel Foucault described a form of 'technology' that would be able to predict the future by processing data.[1] Likewise, this technology will allow us to simulate the potential of an urban site in a more dynamic way than static planning,

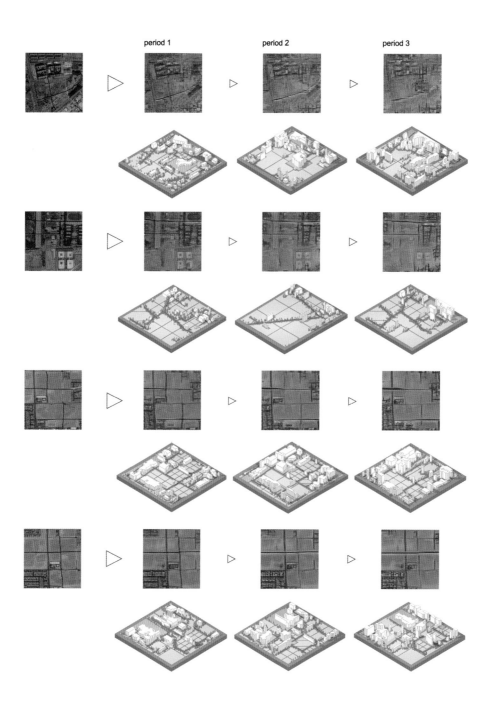

by generating a range of potential outcomes depending on a variety of different factors.

In addition, if a planning proposal is fixed at a certain moment, it is incapable of showing any potential further development. It therefore has a limited capacity to display detailed information or potential variations, or to generate further discussion. With the benefit of prior knowledge and an understanding of the past development of the site, however, a person (or machine) can bring a more comprehensive perspective to the planning process. Moreover, a method that helps predict land-development patterns will also help to promote a more sustainable approach to urban planning.

Recent advances in AI-based probabilistic modelling offer the opportunity to implement this method.

AI has been used to explore the processing of data from images since the turn of the century. Over the past 10 years in particular, AI-based techniques have been used increasingly to explore applications based on high-resolution images, and this trend shows no signs of stopping. Convoluted neural networks (CNNs) and GANs have been used to generate paintings that have been sold at auction,[2] to blend photos, to enhance the resolution of images, to translate images to text, and for many other applications. To this end, the urban planning problem mentioned above is based on two systems: an identification model and an Urban-GAN model.

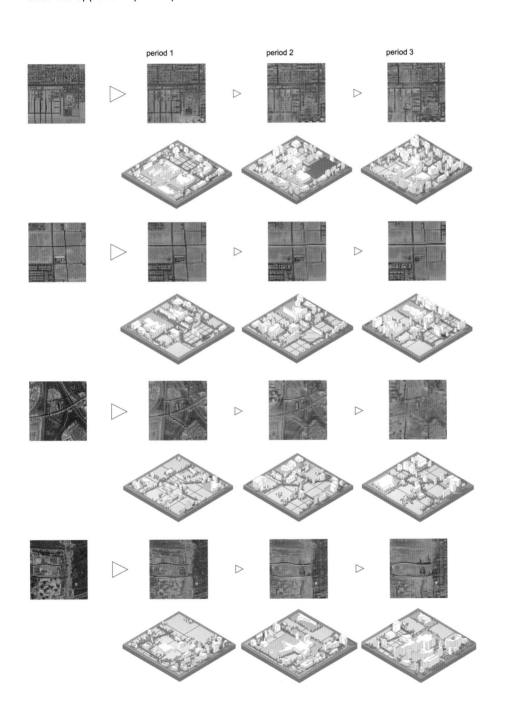

period 1 period 2 period 3

XKool Technology, Sample collections of masterplan schemes over a continuous period, 2021

The road layout (first column) is first defined. This then triggers the generative model to project the sequential changes in the surrounding land on a 2D masterplan year by year (columns 2 to 4). These masterplans are then transformed into 3D format.

Structured Elements Identification

Satellite imagery is a key source of information because it can identify what elements are present (buildings, plantations and streets) and show how these change over periods of time. So the first task in the planning process is to build an identification model to distinguish these elements and extract geometric information. For this reason, the identification model is based on data from a series of satellite images spanning several years, which can express the continuous development and change over time of the site in question.

The identification model needs to be trained with structured 'semantic' data. Semantics are usually expressed in the form of characters and/or numbers. This simple representation provides important information to allow the digital object to be processed, allowing the elements represented in images (or in other unstructured data, such as audio, video and weather data) to be understood.

Of course, images also have their inherent internal data structure, such as pixels expressed in the form of a mathematical matrix, but 'unstructured' here refers specifically to data structures whose meaning is difficult for machines to extract and understand through conventional procedures or methods.[3]

Satellite imagery is unstructured data, hence a series of geometric datasets with specific labels, such as 'site boundary', 'building geometry', 'traffic network', 'green space' and 'waterscape' are used as training materials for the identification model. This allows the model to

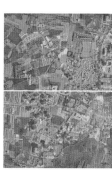

XKool Technology,
Continuous sampling of satellite
images of several cities,
2021

The satellite images record the changes in
land use over a four-year period, and serve as
resourceful data for observing and learning
development patterns using AI.

identify meaningful geometrical elements from satellite images. These labelled data sets are open-source, further ensuring that they match the position and scale of the satellite imagery.

The output of the identification model with clear elements and period labels are then used to train the Urban-GAN model. The machine learns the relationship between the structured geometric elements and the evolutionary sequence based on the learning rules established by humans, but the knowledge it obtains is not directly understandable by humans (it is difficult to directly understand from hundreds of thousands of codes). Nevertheless, it can still ensure that the machine has the ability to predict potential land development over multiple periods of time.

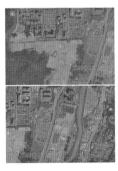

Masterplan Generation in Sequences

An important aspect of site planning is space allocation or building layout. Due to its complexity, this design process is difficult to automate. In addition to the multiple objectives set by the owner, multiple constraints such as planning regulations also need to be met, which affect the street block geometry, building height and width, sunlight coverage and setbacks.

Although the purpose of this exercise is to avoid explicitly programming the above constraints, a more specific type of GAN, Urban-GAN, is used in this generative model to interpret the relationship between the structured data in each period. More specifically, the relationship between the location and shape of the building is mainly learned through the surrounding data accumulated year by year.

It is important to establish the layout of the traffic network before the building layout, because it defines the boundary and potential building plot. The AI model therefore allows human planners to first define the main roads or streets using a satellite image (unlike the training set) by simply delineating it, whether it is on the periphery or within the site. This is then used to trigger the AI generation model to generate a sequence of three time-based, two-dimensional masterplans based on the knowledge it has learned from earlier satellite images. The growth pattern learned in the model will first try to fill the vacant area represented in the satellite image by adding new architectural forms and other elements.

Although the model learns from the past, it does not completely imitate its training data. The 'noise' gene embedded in the generative model allows it to deviate from the original model[4] to a greater or lesser extent, depending on the parameters. This improvisational and random play gives it a degree of creative freedom. However this can be controlled so that it can continuously and steadily generate a range of potential solutions. The final decision still lies in the hands of humans.

XKool Technology,
Respective structured element identified on satellite images,
2021

On the left (from top to bottom), useful information includes waterscape, traffic network, building and greenery, which can be identified on the initial unstructured satellite images. Later, each geometry layer is extracted and given respective semantics labels, as represented on the right.

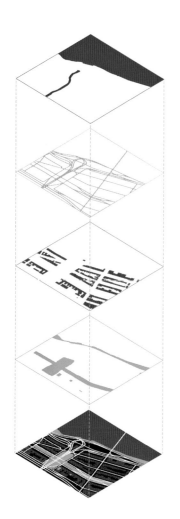

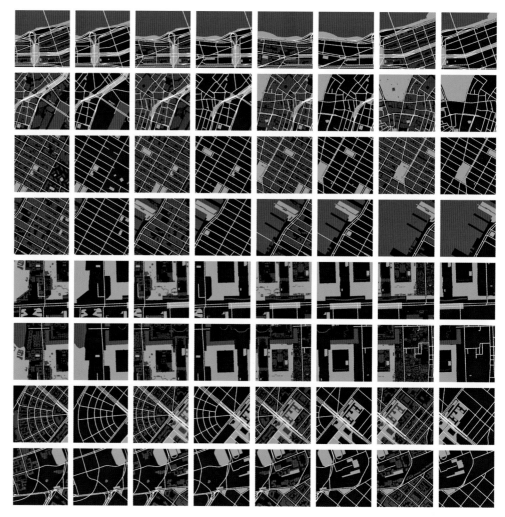

The masterplans that are generated follow the structured information defined by the previous identification model. Some of this structured data is then represented in 3D to make it easier to understand.

Towards Public Participation

Urban-GANs can play important roles in the urban planning process, especially in the early stages of design, such as predicting the potential development of the land based on the various possible road configurations. On the other hand, this modelling process is accessible not only for professional planners, but also for the general public because it is so easy to use. This encourages participation in the planning process, despite the lack of any specialist knowledge.

Besides the structured geometry data mentioned above, other information such as population size, points of interest and noise levels can also be used as training data and to control the parameters of this generative urban planning model. ⌀

XKool Technology,
2D masterplan output visualised in 3D models,
2021

Structured components in the generated 2D masterplan are transformed into 3D models to make them easier to understand, with their building heights calculated automatically.

Notes
1. Michel Foucault, *Security, Territory, Population: Lectures at the Collège De France, 1977–78*, Palgrave Macmillan (New York), 2009, pp 14–27.
2. 'Is Artificial Intelligence Set to Become Art's Next Medium?', Christies.com, 12 December 2018: www.christies.com/features/A-collaboration-between-two-artists-one-human-one-a-machine-9332-1.aspx
3. IBM Cloud Education, 'Structured vs Unstructured Data: What's the Difference?', Ibm.com, 29 June 2021: www.ibm.com/cloud/blog/structured-vs-unstructured-data.
4. 'The Generator': https://developers.google.com/machine-learning/gan/generator.

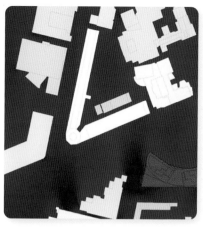

Theodoros Galanos
and Angelos Chronis

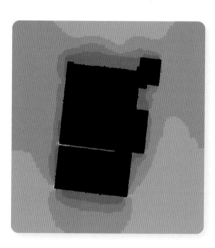
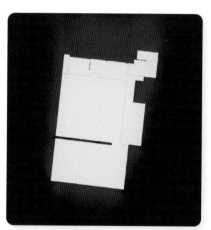

TIME FOR CHANGE – THE INFRARED REVOLUTION

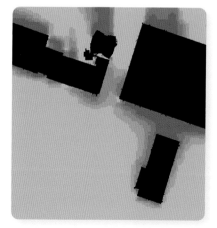

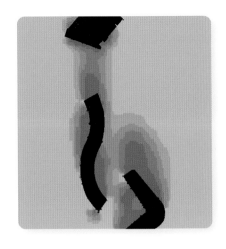
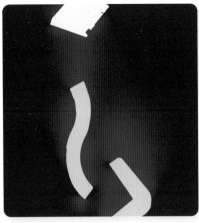

Theodoros Galanos and Angelos Chronis,
Intelligent Framework for
Resilient Design (InFraRed),
City Intelligence Lab,
Austrian Institute of Technology,
Vienna,
2021

Performance prediction and respective error plots.
Design performance (bottom) and error estimates
(top) offer users of InFraRed technology transparency
and increase confidence in the use of the platform.

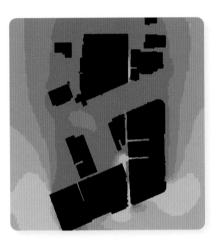
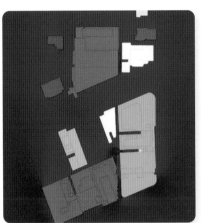

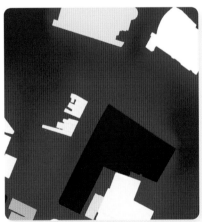

HOW AI-DRIVEN TOOLS CAN REINVENT DESIGN FOR EVERYONE

The synthesis of human design inspiration and serendipity and the use of digital tools has been the aim of much architectural research over the last 50 years. **Theodoros Galanos and Angelos Chronis** from the Austrian Institute of Technology in Vienna describe the AI tools they have developed to achieve real-time, dynamic representation of design performance and design intent.

There is a long history of applied research into intelligent, mixed-initiative design systems in architecture. Some of the earliest works were by Christopher Alexander with HIDESC3[1] in the 1960s, and Nicholas Negroponte and Yona Friedman with Urban5[2] and YONA[3] in the 1970s. These tools explored computer-aided architectural design, with an emphasis on human-machine interaction, and the goal of developing a collaborative relationship between human designer and machine, and establishing creative and educational dialogue. Negroponte attempted to increase the machine's 'awareness' of the user's preferences and enable what was called 'mutual and successful interruptability'. The aim was to democratise design, freeing the user from the 'patronage' of the architect, by enabling non-experts to make their own designs, articulate their needs and desires and bear the risk of failure. User participation was a major focus, building an interface between infrastructure and the user's ever-changing needs across personalised design problems.

Despite this activity between 1960 and 1980, few steps forward have been made in the last 40 years. Interfaces used in practice today are almost devoid of these mixed-initiative design elements and are tied into specific software rather than influenced by new theories and developments in generative design and human-computer interaction. Instead, we have to turn to the gaming AI field to find fresh, innovative applications. Sentient Sketchbook,[4] a game-level authoring tool that allows the design of map sketches via an intuitive interface, gives real-time feedback of evaluated metrics and suggestions of alternative designs to its users, providing a bidirectional feedback between tool and designer. Tanagra[5] allows designers to make and play platform levels that are engaging and meet their expectations, and Ropossum[6] incorporates designer input when creating designs and automatically checks and optimises for playability. All highlight the focus of modern mixed-initiative design tools: allowing the user to influence the process of design, in real time. By striving to be practical in real-life settings and in creating valid designs – an important consideration for architects and engineers – they are great examples of how to increase the adoption of mixed-initiative generative design.

The Intelligent Framework for Resilient Design (InFraRed), developed by the City Intelligence Lab at the Austrian Institute of Technology, leverages these insights in a tool that positions the human designer at its core. Building from the recent success of deep learning, it uses pre-trained, surrogate models of urban performance to enable real-time interaction between design performance and design intent.[7] The aim is to revisit the earlier but visionary approaches of the 1960s, but armed with the comprehensive and powerful direct-learning arsenal of today.

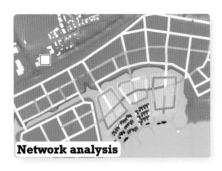

Network analysis

Traffic analysis (transit, cars, pedestrians)

Commute time to work

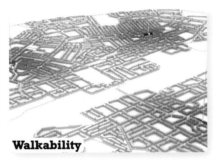

Walkability

Theodoros Galanos and Angelos Chronis,
Intelligent Framework for
Resilient Design (InFraRed),
City Intelligence Lab,
Austrian Institute of Technology,
Vienna, 2021

InFraRed's suite of services provides a comprehensive urban performance evaluation toolbox, with deep-learning models giving real-time feedback for time-consuming simulations.

AI-accelerated sunlight-hours prediction

Accessibility

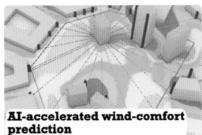

AI-accelerated wind-comfort prediction

AI-accelerated noise pollution prediction

Footfall

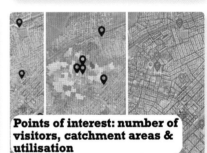

Points of interest: number of visitors, catchment areas & utilisation

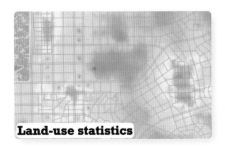

Land-use statistics

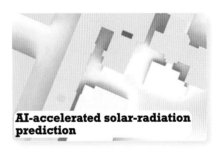

AI-accelerated solar-radiation prediction

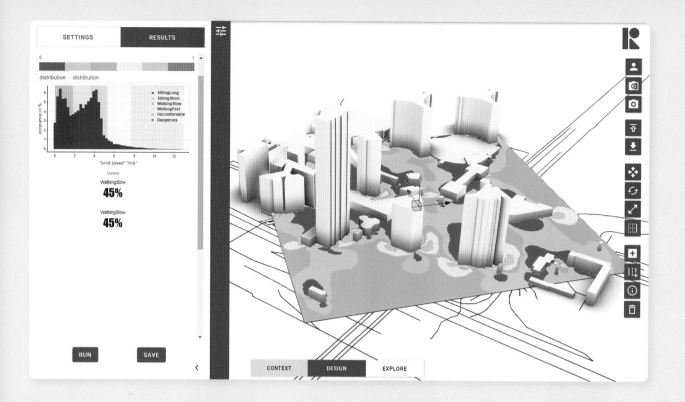

Theodoros Galanos and Angelos Chronis,
Intelligent Framework for Resilient Design (InFraReD),
City Intelligence Lab,
Austrian Institute of Technology, Vienna, 2021

above: Wind-comfort simulation prediction on InFraReD's cloud platform. Users can create global projects online, and design and evaluate their performance in real time.

below: InFraReD's deep-learning networks are trained from large simulation datasets produced using industry-standard simulation methods.

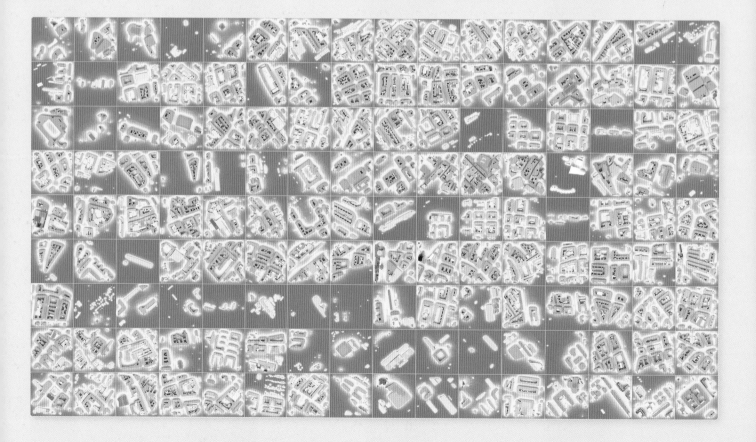

Time and Design Practice

Theophrastus, the successor to Aristotle in the Peripatetic School, famously said: 'Time is the most valuable thing a man can spend.' In a domain where value is everything, and counted in time, it is astonishing how much of it we spend on certain tasks. Time, of course, is only one dimension. The most challenging design problems are multidisciplinary, complex assemblages that involve a vast array of expertise required to solve them. Time and expertise together define what we can do, but in many ways they also define the limit of what we do, at least in practice. The lack of solutions to the problem of time and expertise effectively limits the potential of most computational design workflows. As a result, our current design processes only scratch the surface of what is possible.

AI is seen by many as a force of automation, a way to replace difficult and repetitive tasks with automated processes that reduce time and labour, and increase value. InFraRed is an AI-driven urban design platform that aims to do more than this, in providing easier access to these complex simulations for all. In doing so, it does not attempt to remove human input, but in fact elevate it, placing it at the core of the design process and allowing a fluid collaboration between designer and machine, grounded on, and driven by, performance. It solves the problem of time by simply bypassing the need for time and time-consuming simulations.

InfraRed is an AI-driven urban-design platform that aims to provide easier access to complex simulations for all

The Intersection Between AI and Design

InFraRed also tackles the problem of expertise required to run and understand such simulations. Its surrogate models can be deployed in any interface and work behind the scenes to generate feedback. They represent a paradigm shift in software design and computation within architecture as the first glimpse of 'Software 2.0' self-contained programs that can be easily deployed and immediately provide valuable design services, in this case performance-driven urban design. This means that expensive, difficult and knowledge-intensive integrations within specialised design software are no longer needed; practitioners can build their own custom solutions around these models. The InFraRed platform, which recently entered its beta stage, is an example of this, but the opportunities to deploy it in downstream applications are endless.

An important consideration when using surrogate models to predict rather than simulate performance is accuracy, which is generally treated as a straightforward, quantifiable measure of a model's predictive capacity, in this case how close the predictions are to an equivalent simulation – the higher the accuracy the better the model. However, accuracy is a much more nuanced phenomenon and needs to be analysed from different practical dimensions.

Preliminary studies have demonstrated that InFraRed appears to have an average mean absolute error between prediction and simulation in the range of 5 to 20 per cent. Given that it allows for a reduction of almost 99.95 per cent of time required for a simulation, this trade-off is satisfactory, especially during concept design. But it is also necessary to expand the notion of accuracy from a single number to a spatially aware metric. Knowing exactly where the model is least accurate matters. InFraRed's error prediction module provides exactly this kind of intelligence by visualising error in a way that allows the user to draw their own inferences and decisions. Another dimension of accuracy that needs to be considered is transparency, which is crucial in new design technology in helping to increase confidence and allow for more meaningful relationships to form between designer and tool.

The final dimension relates to the idea of the design space versus a singular design. Real-time prediction fuels a new kind of design focused towards design exploration and discovery, building on our ability to analyse vast design spaces within a matter of hours. In this situation, accuracy becomes the horizon of the exploratory process and can be inferred by the 'decisions' the model makes as searches for well-performing designs in different scenarios. Accuracy is then transformed from an output metric to a process of learning as the designer and tool, hand in hand, explore large design spaces, generating and extracting design intelligence.

Building on the potential of quality diversity, InfraRed aims to develop open-ended design environments where large spaces can be populated and explored, paving the way for innovative interpretation

A Step Forward: From Design Tools to Design Intelligence

InFraRed introduces a number of innovations that change the way we approach design today. However, the vision of AI-driven tools as forces of automation and efficiency is not bold enough. We need to consider these technologies as transformative and work out the implications of what that means and how they impact design. InFraRed hopes to do this by shifting the focus from optimisation to exploration. Building on the potential of quality diversity,[8] the aim is to develop open-ended design environments where large spaces can be populated and explored, paving the way for innovative interpretation that moves from *what* happens within different regions to *why* differences emerge, and what

InFraRed will utilise quality diversity, a collection of population-based evolutionary methods, for exploration of complex design spaces, across dimensions chosen by the designer. Here, one such method, called MAP-Elites, is used to construct a map of well-performing designs, providing a more intuitive understanding of the design space.

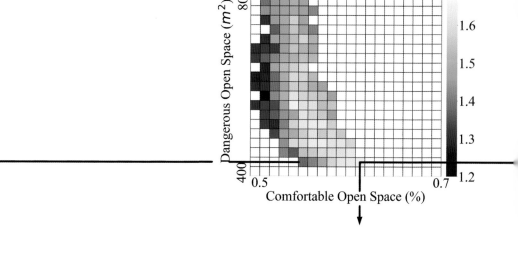

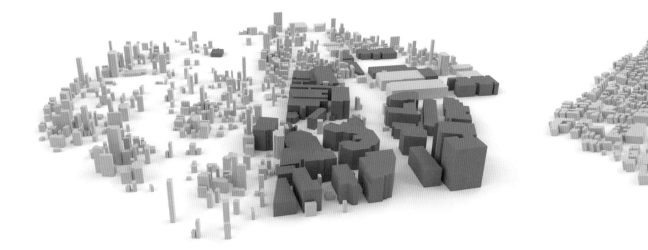

the crucial parameters are that drive them. Being able to cluster designs in different ways allows the training of new models to embed important dimensions to generate new, well-performing designs that create performance-driven generators. Uncovering the latent structure of design spaces also allows us to traverse them and to visualise how design parameters and performance shift and change at each step. It is the coming together of all these new capabilities that enables this process of generating, extracting, articulating and communicating the novel insight at the core of design intelligence. InFraRed aims to be exactly that, a stage where design intelligence can be produced as a commodity in itself that allows users of the platform to learn and develop better intuitions, and a stronger understanding of the relationship between urban design and performance. ∆

Notes
1. Christopher Alexander, *HIDECS 3: Four Computer Programs for the Hierarchical Decomposition of Systems which Have an Associated Linear Graph*, Research report. Massachusetts Institute of Technology (Cambridge, MA), 1963: https://nopinegoma.thebookpapery.icu/hidecs-3-book-9316bd.php.
2. Nicholas Negroponte and Leon Groissier, *URBAN 5: An OnLine Urban Design Partner*, IBM Report (Cambridge, MA), 1967.
3. Guy Weinzapfel and Nicholas Negroponte, 'Architecture-by-Yourself: An Experiment with Computer Graphics for House Design', *ACM SIGGRAPH Computer Graphics* 10 (2), 1976, pp 74–8.
4. Antonios Liapis, Georgios N Yannakakis and Julian Togelius, 'Sentient Sketchbook: Computer-aided Game Level Authoring', in *Proceedings of the 8th Conference on the Foundations of Digital Games* (FDG), Chania, Crete, May 2013, pp 213–20.
5. Gillian Smith, Jim Whitehead and Michael Mateas, 'Tanagra: An Intelligent Level Design Assistant for 2D Platformers', in *Proceedings of the Sixth AAAI Conference on Artificial Intelligence and Interactive Digital Entertainment (AIIDE)*, Stanford, California, October 2010, pp 223–4.
6. Mohammad Shaker, Noor Shaker and Julian Togelius, 'Ropossum: An Authoring Tool for Designing, Optimizing and Solving Cut the Rope Levels', in *Proceedings of the 9th AAAI Conference on Artificial Intelligence and Interactive Digital Entertainment*, 2013, pp 215–16.
7. Theodoros Galanos and Angelos Chronis, 'A Deep-Learning Approach to Real-Time Solar Radiation Prediction', in Imdat As and Prithwish Basu (eds), *The Routledge Companion to Artificial Intelligence in Architecture*, Routledge (London), 2021, pp 224–31.
8. Theodoros Galanos *et al*, 'ARCH-Elites: Quality-Diversity for Urban Design', arxiv.org, 2021: https://arxiv.org/pdf/2104.08774v1.pdf.

Cyborg Liv

ganic

ing

Maria Kuptsova,
Lidar scanning,
Synthetic
Landscape Lab,
University
of Innsbruck,
Austria,
2021

Ubiquitous, systemic and
intelligent technologies become
an equal actor in the ecosystem
in which we live. Neural networks
and algorithms that reconstruct
three-dimensional space using
cameras and lidars are the senses
of intelligent agents that inhabit
the cyborganic city.

Transdisciplinary artist and researcher **Maria Kuptsova** works in the interstices between organic and digital systems. As she seeks new ways to design landscapes that are a rich mix of biological processes and computational algorithms and tools, she generates what she calls 'cyborganic' or 'bio-machinic' architectural languages.

Our concept of nature has evolved from a romantic garden of Eden to a 'cyborganic' form of living understood as a 'natural-technical continuum'.[1] Non-human agents, such as machinic algorithms, transgenic plants and planetary viruses are equal actors within the hybrid reality we live in. There is strong potential for an explosion of new design methods taking form through synthetic biology and AI. However, contemporary design computation is still centred on humans and structured by our prejudices. Can a design technique be developed that could shape a new form of communication between human and non-human agents,[2] replacing the anthropocentric approach with the design of cyborganic living systems?

SYNTHETIC FORMS OF INTELLIGENCE
Biological organisms operate with their own biases and modes of reasoning. Strata within the landscape encode and store knowledge about microclimates, microchemical compositions and multispecies interactions.[3] The behavioural models of fungi, bacteria, insects and animals can be understood as a form of intelligence which acts within a seemingly 'alien' realm. For example, the microscopic patterns of a plant contain information about the intelligent mechanisms of photosynthesis, growth, water and food distribution. Embedding the organisational principles of an organic material into a digital system would allow a form of hybrid materiality to be designed that might host biological intelligence within a digital structure.

Machinic intelligence has the capacity to search, generate and process information more efficiently than human beings. Machine learning might therefore be considered as an instrument of 'knowledge magnification that helps to perceive features, patterns, and correlations through vast spaces of data beyond human reach'.[4] Biological models can frame new biases for machinic operations. The intelligence of an organic system, which can be decoded by reading large databases of biological patterns and behaviours, could potentially influence a technological system with its own evolutionary algorithm. This conversation between biological and technological systems thus frames a metalanguage[5] that could be considered as a form of synthetic intelligence. Its structure would therefore be a metasyntax for the design of a cyborganic living system where biological and technological agency become an inherent part of the design process.

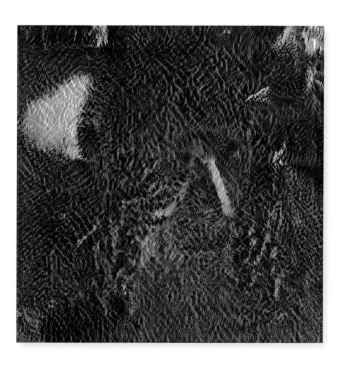

Xuehan Tong and Bo Liu,
Style GAN Model Trained on Satellite Data,
Urban Design MArch,
Research Cluster 16,
Bartlett School of Architecture,
University College London (UCL),
London, 2021

Technology embedded in multiple objects within a landscape allows new regimes and metabolism to evolve. Through sensors and intelligent technologies, the complexity of flows, behaviours and patterns embedded within the planetarian metabolism can be decoded.

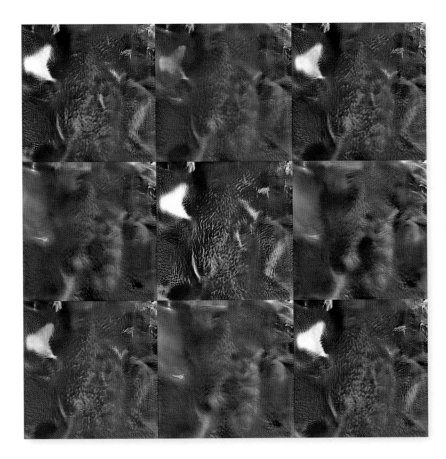

New forms of cyborganic living evolve both technological and biological systems. A synthetic environment can be understood as a planetary-scale biocomputer capable of storing, transmitting and sharing data and knowledge.

IMPLEMENTATION OF SYNTHETIC INTELLIGENCE INTO DESIGN PROTOCOLS

The cyborganic, bio-artificial sculpture Arbor, developed in the Synthetic Landscape Lab at the University of Innsbruck, is a high-resolution, 3D-printed system designed by both human and non-human forms of intelligence. It demonstrates a machine-learning-based design technique that is contextualised in a new form of material and formal articulation with the aim of imparting biological intelligence into inorganic objects and synthetic environments. The project outlines an approach for reading the intelligence of an organic timber structure using machine-learning algorithms, as well as rethinking the life cycle of wood, proposing a bio-artificial system that is alive in a cybernetic sense.

Wood is widely used in building construction because of its mechanical, environmental, economical, acoustic, elastic, thermal, hygroscopic and aesthetic properties. However, its heterogeneous properties in its living state are usually considered to be somewhat problematic. In order to study the material organisation of wood, Arbor uses a large database of the botanical characteristics of different wood species developed by the ArchiWood project.[6] Micro images of 995 species were collected and analysed with different contrasting techniques. The microscopic images of wood cuts reveal the distribution of vessels and fibres generating a continuous lightweight tissue with varying degrees of density and porosity. These pores cause a strong molecular attraction between water and the cellulose in wood. The anisotropic properties are crucial characteristics of the timber structure, representing its constant and reciprocal interaction with the surrounding environment. These qualities, usually considered negative side-effects, can be rethought and reused in the design of artificial living systems that can develop functional capacities through such interaction with their environment.

The Arbor project proposes the use of generative adversarial networks (GANs) as a method of extracting principles of material organisation from an existing database of timber structures for the purpose of developing volumetric models. The main advantage of GANs is their ability to generate new unseen imagery based on given data, allowing such networks to interpolate between selected pairs of images by generating intermediate steps. During the training process, GAN architecture forms a latent space, which can be imagined as the space of the network's knowledge. A series of points can be created on a linear path between two points in the latent space to set up a 'latent vector'.[7]

For this research, the StyleGAN2 generative adversarial network was chosen as the most advanced and most studied in architecture. A series of experiments were conducted to train it on a range of wood cuts at different scales. The transverse cut magnified 200 times was selected as the most consistent, and this model was used to visualise the internal and external morphology of the material organisation of the timber with the latent-vector interpolation translated into the Z axis of the volumetric structure. In this process, basic geometrical data describing the anatomical properties of the Arbor timber structure

Maria Kuptsova,
Arbor,
Synthetic Landscape Lab,
University of Innsbruck,
2021

above: A volumetric model is created from point-cloud data extracted from cross-sections of the wooden structure. A network of curves and surfaces describes geometric data about the anatomical properties of the wood structure.

below: StyleGAN model trained on timber structure depictions, tangential section cut, magnification x200. With the ability of GANs to read patterns and imagine new formations, multiple latent layers of GAN algorithms can be used to extract the behavioural model of a timber structure.

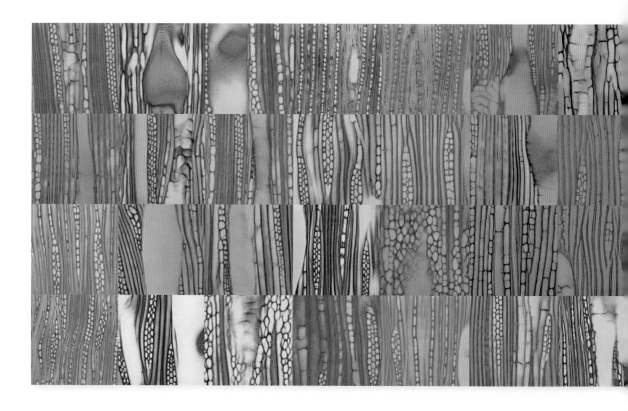

In the Arbor project, a
timber-based filament
was used as a 3D-printing
material, suggesting a
new regenerative life cycle
of matter from the wood
in its living state to a
recycled wooden material

as transformable meshes were extracted. This network of curves and surfaces describes the distribution of material as a behavioural pattern. The volumetric model was formed based on point-cloud data generated from transverse timber cuts. This discontinuous volumetric dataset contains information on material organisation principles such as the allocation of stiff and soft materials within the structure, fibre-density gradients, as well as variations in hydrophilic properties.

Fabrication technologies such as additive manufacturing allow for the development of adaptive fabrication methods informed by research into material behaviour. In the Arbor project, a timber-based filament was used as a 3D-printing material, suggesting a new regenerative life cycle of matter from the wood in its living state to a recycled wooden material. The use of an industrial 3D printer, Wasp, allowed for material experimentation at a larger scale. These fabrication methods, as well as the introduction of machine-learning-based design techniques, suggest scenarios where a cyborganic wooden structure could be artificially grown by means of intelligent technologies, challenging the processes of growth, decay and ontogenesis and introducing a cyborganic living object in a 'synthetic landscape choreography' driven by non-human biases, co-designed and receptive to interaction with human, technological and biological systems. Δ

Notes
1. Erich Hörl, 'A Thousand Ecologies: the Process of Cybernetization and General Ecology', in Diedrich Diederichsen and Anselm Franke (eds), *The Whole Earth: California and the Disappearance of the Outside*, Sternberg Press (Berlin), 2013, p 128.
2. Claudia Pasquero and Marco Poletto, 'Deep Green', *topos* 112, 2020, p 27.
3. Marco Poletto, 'The Urbansphere: Architecture in the Age of Ubiquitous Computing', PhD thesis, RMIT University, Melbourne, 2018.
4. Matteo Pasquinelli and Vladen Joler, 'The Nooscope Manifested: AI as Instrument of Knowledge Extractivism', *AI & Society*, 2020: https://link.springer.com/article/10.1007/s00146-020-01097-6#auth-Vladan-Joler.
5. Gregory Bateson, *Mind and Nature: A Necessary Unity*, EP Dutton (New York), 1979, p 117, box 6.
6. https://archiwood.cirad.fr/.
7. Tero Karras, Samuli Laine and Timo Aila, 'A Style-Based Generator Architecture for Generative Adversarial Networks', arxiv.org, 29 March 2019, p 8.

Maria Kuptsova,
Arbor,
'Potenziale 3' exhibition,
Innsbruck, Austria,
2021

Arbor is a bio-artificial sculpture that is alive in the cybernetic sense. It challenges the processes of growth, decay and ontogenesis through the introduction of machine-learning-based design techniques and the implementation of regenerative life cycles of matter from a living state to recycled materials.

Matias del Campo and Neil Leach

UNLEASHING NEW CREATIVITIES

In his book *Space, Time and Architecture* (1941),[1] Sigfried Giedion describes the emergence of a new tradition in architecture. He articulates how Modernism was propelled and fuelled by technological insights that triggered a response in artistic production. From there, only a short jump to architecture was required, as suddenly architects began to understand – through the arts – how these novel technological possibilities sparked ideas that liberated space, created open plans and reduced architecture to an abstract expression. A parallel can be made with the current rise of a new paradigm in architecture shaped by AI. Neural Art paved the way to the possibilities inherent in the abilities of neural networks to crunch through inhumanly large datasets and extract the salient features latent in this data. AI turns data into information that contains enough familiar features to be recognisable in return as architecture. But can AI also be creative?

A number of commentators, including Margaret Boden, Marcus du Sautoy and Arthur Miller, believe that AI can indeed be creative.[2] Melanie Mitchell, however, argues that in order to be creative, you must be aware of the fact that you are being creative.[3] As such, AI cannot be creative until it has achieved consciousness, or artificial general intelligence (AGI). Meanwhile, artist and self-proclaimed 'neurographer' Mario Klingemann believes that it is the artist and not the technology that is being creative: 'If you heard someone playing the piano, would you ask "Is the piano the artist?" No. So, same thing here. Just because it is a complicated mechanism, it doesn't change the roles.'[4]

A more relevant question, then, might be whether AI can help architects to be creative, and be understood as a prosthesis to the human imagination, a form of extended intelligence that opens up new creative ways of operating.

The projects here imaginatively address the theme of creativity. Eduard Haiman, chief design officer of Habidatum in Moscow, combines general adversarial networks (GANs) with human intervention to generate his mesmerising 'Endless Skyscraper' series. Associate Professor Gabriel Esquivel and Master's student Shane Bugni at Texas A&M University, and Jean Jaminet, Assistant Professor at Kent State University, Ohio, show us how GANs can also be used to open up history in interesting new ways by creatively reinterpreting the drawings of Italian Mannerist artist Sebastiano Serlio. Alisa Andrasek, Professor of Design Innovation Technology at RMIT University in Melbourne, eloquently shows how a new form of creativity is emerging at the threshold between humans and machines with the spinning swarms of agents that drive her *Cloud Pergola* installation. For their exquisite Dream Estate project, Damjan Jovanovic and Lidija Kljakovic of lifeforms.io combine AI with Unreal Engine and Houdini. As Hao Zheng, doctoral candidate at the University of Pennsylvania in Philadelphia, points out in his brilliant project on dragonfly wings, AI can also be used creatively with graphic statics to understand structural behaviours. Kyle Steinfeld, Associate Professor at the University of California, Berkeley, uses StyleGANs to reinterpret a Greco-Roman sculptural relief.

Taken together, these projects offer a glimpse of the possibilities afforded by AI. It is not simply that AI itself can generate novel outcomes – it also has the capacity to open up novel modes of creative practice.

FollyFeastLab (Yara Feghali and Viviane El-Kmati), Mediterranean Sea Diaries, 2020

A playful, accessible and inclusive virtual-reality version of a UN climate convention on e-waste, Mediterranean Sea Diaries by LA-based experimental design studio FollyFeastLab uses AI for behavioural simulation and object placement.

Notes
1. Sigfried Giedion, *Space, Time and Architecture: The Growth of a New Tradition*, Harvard University Press (Cambridge, MA), 2009. First published in 1941.
2. Margaret Boden, 'Computer Models of Creativity', *Handbook of Creativity*, Cambridge University Press (Cambridge), 1998, pp 351–72; Marcus du Sautoy, *The Creativity Code: Art and Innovation in the Age of AI*, Harvard University Press (Cambridge, MA), 2019; Arthur Miller, *The Artist in the Machine: The World of AI-Powered Creativity*, MIT Press (Cambridge, MA), 2019.
3. Melanie Mitchell, *Artificial Intelligence: A Guide for Thinking Humans*, Farrar, Straus and Giroux (New York), 2019, p 272.
4. Martin Dean, 'Artist Mario Klingemann on Artificial Intelligence, Technology and our Future', interview with the artist, Sothebys.com, 25 February 2019: www.sothebys.com/en/articles/artist-mario-klingemann-on-artificial-intelligence-art-tech-and-our-future.

Endlessskyscraper

'Endlessskyscraper' is a series of experiments that involve aesthetic principles and form-finding processes that combine human design with an artificial perception that emerges out of the nature of neural networks. The outcome is a series of images of towers generated by a generative adversarial network (GAN) that uses the collective memory of architectural plans that are then rendered using procedural materials. The project is an attempt to fuse two forms of architectural representation: one developed using a human understanding of space that includes orthogonal perception, gravity, tectonics and cultural reference, and the other an interpretation created by AI that knows nothing about the human mind, physical laws or building codes.

Seamless and Continuous

A neural network perceives reality differently to how the human brain understands it. If the human brain has adapted throughout evolution to categorise objects,[1] a GAN exhibits seamlessly continuous effects that emerge naturally through interpolation.[2] During training, a GAN forms an abstract, multidimensional, latent space that contains features that a human cannot interpret directly. Latent space includes all possible variations that can be generated within that space. To draw an analogy with neurophysiology, the structures of the human brain include all memories that can be called to mind. An interpolation between these two coordinates creates a gradual, sequential change.[3] Seamless and continuous effects emerge as higher-order effects related to the interpolating properties of the latent space. Together with the lack of interpretability of latent space features, these effects highlight the fundamental differences between artificial and human perception.

Eduard Haiman,
Frame of Eponymous Animation,
'Endlessskyscraper' series,
2021

An infinity tower is generated by using a StyleGAN2 neural network trained on architectural plans. The tower is dissected heightwise using a spiral surface to visually fuse exterior and interior spatial patterns. The animation and the spiral-wise volume allow the structure to be perceived not as a dichotomy between inside and out, but as a volumetric union system generated by AI that knows nothing about such human concepts.

Eduard Haiman,
Form-generation diagram,
'Endlessskyscraper' series,
2021

Drawings of walls were generated using a StyleGAN2 neural network trained on architectural plans. Each floor is built by combining 60 drawings that gradually change. The spiral cut allows views of the tower interiors and emphasises both cycles and infinity.

Eduard Haiman,
Crumbly Stripes on Rich Black,
'Endlesssskyscraper' series,
2021

The experiment uses coloured stripes at slightly different angles. They allow us to see the infinity tower volume not as a stack of the architectural plans generated by the neural network, but as nuances of the tower surface brought out by the crossing and overlaying of the coloured stripes. Received cuts simultaneously destroy the unity of the tower volume visually and, together with distorted 3D space (where the tower is placed), detach perception from the architecture's orthogonality.

Field Architecture

Human-made architecture defines spaces and structures using means that are familiar to the human consciousness. Architects therefore use taxonomy-based diagrams[4] and tend to build hierarchies based on functions, roles or spatial relations that might change over time but persist throughout history.[5] The desire to build gradients of space that form endless fields instead of structures drives the 'Endlesssskyscraper' project. The continuity and seamless properties that emerge in latent space directly follow properties in the mathematical field. Stan Allen's principles of field conditions[6] thus arise from the GAN's internal structure instead of analogies or algorithmic simulations of field properties.

The Aesthetics of Blended Perception

'Endlesssskyscraper' uses a neural network trained on drawings of architectural plans that reflect social and natural circumstances and the structure of the human mind at the time. The networks' seamlessly continuous properties meet with human-made architectural patterns to give birth to a new blended digital form that is unfinished and unstable, and can potentially be translated into architecture.

Digital form demands visual properties that supply the GAN's alien behaviour and contradict human or physical logic. The project explores human perception of volumetric properties and composition features and converts them into procedural visualisation algorithms imprinted in virtual sculptures, animations or posters.

Notes
1. Henri Cohen and Claire Lefebvre (eds), *Handbook of Categorization in Cognitive Science*, Elsevier (Amsterdam), 2nd edn, 2017, p 196.
2. Tero Karras, Samuli Laine and Timo Aila, 'A Style-Based Generator Architecture for Generative Adversarial Networks', arxiv.org, 2019, pp 1, 6:https://arxiv.org/pdf/1812.04948.pdf.
3. Jason Brownlee, 'How to Explore the GAN Latent Space When Generating Faces', Machine Learning Mastery, 1 September 2020: https://machinelearningmastery.com/how-to-interpolate-and-perform-vector-arithmetic-with-faces-using-a-generative-adversarial-network/.
4. Mark Garcia (ed), *The Diagrams of Architecture: AD Reader*, John Wiley & Sons (Chichester), 2010, pp 18–19.
5. Michael Hensel, Christopher Hight and Achim Menges, 'En route: Towards a Discourse on Heterogeneous Space Beyond Modernist Space-Time and Post-modernist Social Geography', *Heterogeneous Space in Architecture*: *Space Reader*, John Wiley & Sons (Chichester), 2009, pp 17–23.
6. Stan Allen, 'From Object to Field: Field Conditions in Architecture and Urbanism', in Hensel, Hight and Menges, *op cit*, pp 119–20.

Eduard Haiman,
Purple Mountain Majestic Foggy Stratums,
'Endlesssskyscraper' series,
2021

The foggy material applied to the infinity tower allows us to look deep inside the architectural volume shaped by the architectural plans generated by the neural network, revealing hidden patterns. It is a visual representation of Stan Allen's principles of field conditions and permeability in architecture.

Gabriel Esquivel, Jean Jaminet and Shane Bugni

```
Gabriel Esquivel, Jean Jaminet and Shane Bugni,
The Serlio Code,
College of Architecture, Texas A&M University,
College Station, Texas,
2021
```

The Serlio Code

Virtual design production has demanded that information be increasingly encoded and decoded by means of image-compression technologies. Since the Renaissance, the discourses of language and drawing and their actuation by the Classical disciplinary treatise have been fundamental to the production of knowledge within the building arts. These early forms of data compression provoke the following reflections on theory and technology as critical counterparts to perception and imagination unique to the discipline of architecture.

The architectural treatise is a technical-literary genre considered to be an essential part of the historical development of architecture. Sebastiano Serlio's *Tutte l'opere d'architettura, et prospetiva* (All the Works on Architecture and Perspective) (1619)[1] was the first treatise to include copious drawings and illustrations as a central feature of the literature, introducing a potent visual dimension to the study of architecture.[2] Serlio's imagery has initiated long-standing discussions about the entanglements between architectural language and the coded operations of orthographic projection drawing. What is fascinating about his experiments is that in applying the codes, he proceeds to vigilantly deviate from them. The results are sometimes defined by the code, where the code and the product are isomorphic. At other times, architectural elements are aberrant or misaligned, which suggests that a latent diagrammatic operation other than the code is at work. Thus, in Serlio we find entrenched the digital code (transposition) within its analogical modulation (transfiguration). These insights into the discordant pairing of the analogue and the digital bring new disciplinary relevance to Serlio's pictorial treatise within current advancements and discussions concerning machine learning.

Examination of aesthetic communication theory provides a conceptual dimension to the ways in which architecture and artificial intelligent systems process information. Significant parallels can be drawn between Gilles Deleuze's account of the diagrammatic modulation in the paintings of Francis Bacon[3] and the analogue-to-digital conversion process performed by image-based neural networks. Similar distorted figures can be discerned in both Bacon's macabre portraits and crude AI-generated faces. In both cases, the diagram produces novel effects and removes any predetermined resemblances that might be implied on the canvas or in the generated image. The mimetic powers of technological data storage and retrieval as well as Serlio's coded operations disclose other aesthetic and formal logics for architecture and its image that exist outside human perception.

Serlio Encoded

The Serlio Code design research project at the College of Architecture, Texas A&M University,[4] examines the illustrated expositions of Sebastiano Serlio through the lens of AI. The intention of this design experimentation is not to simulate Serlio's illustrations, but rather modulate their qualities and problematise their 2D to 3D translation beyond the rules of representation and orthographic projection. AI models and equivocal digital workflows produce outputs that exhibit distortions and fragmentations through recursive computational procedures, depositing layers of visual and semantic content in each successive operation. In returning Serlio's drawings to object status, the operative façade and column models illustrated here involve augmenting and interpreting layered GANs that drive an integrated

opposite: Digital rendering of an object created through synthesising cross-section cuts taken from Serlio's columns (artwork Austin White).

below: Style-transfer digital rendering generated from an unrolled UV map trained on Serlio's drawings (artwork Spencer Young).

A full-scale physical artefact in a façade configuration that shows distortions and fragmentations of recursive computational procedures.

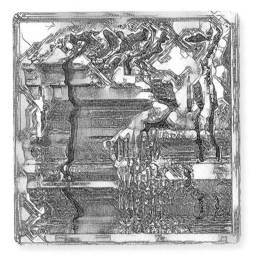

A full-scale physical artefact with extruded polystyrene foam, drywall compound and acrylic paint in a façade configuration that combines CNC milling with manual sculpting and finishing.

parametric process of three-dimensionalisation. The hyper-mediated status of the drawing is further communicated through full-scale physical artefacts that combine 3D printing and CNC milling fabrication techniques with analogue procedures of casting, sculpting and decorative painting. These tools and methods surrender established roles of authorship, complicate normative and predictable linear design processes, and resist conventional orthographic translations from drawing to building.

Machine learning defies the notions of consistency, semantics and representation that have defined architectural language since the Renaissance. The examination of Serlio's illustrated volumes through the lens of artificial intelligence stimulates alternative modes of perception and provides disciplinary perspective on our technological circumstances, alluding to new languages and forms of expression yet to be discovered. The Serlio Code is an ongoing project that further reinforces architecture's command of contemporary techno-cultural discourses regarding medium, communication and agency.

Notes
1. Sebastiano Serlio, *Tutte l'opere d'architettura,* ed Giovanni Domenico Scamozzi (reprint of 1619 edn), Gregg Press (Ridgewood, NJ), 1964.
2. Francesco Benelli, 'The Life and Work of Sebastiano Serlio', *Digital Serlio Project*, Avery Architectural & Fine Arts Library, 2018: https://library.columbia.edu/content/dam/libraryweb/locations/avery/classics/Serlio/Benelli3.pdf.
3. Gilles Deleuze, *Francis Bacon: The Logic of Sensation* [1981], trans Daniel W Smith, Continuum (New York), 2003, pp 99–110.
4. Funded by Kent State University College of Architecture and Environmental Design.

Cloud Pergola

Alisa Andrasek

Superperformance in highly complex biological systems stems largely from high-resolution articulation and repatterning of building blocks at a micro scale. Everything successful in nature, science and technology operates at a very high resolution. Cutting-edge science is shifting from rationalism to computationalism, moving away from compressed models of knowledge such as mathematical equations and ideals reflecting the Modernist mindset, and instead deriving new knowledge through pattern recognition from a sea of data. It is a shift from formal procedures to big data and machine learning.

This new scientific and technological context offers opportunities for accelerated architectural synthesis, where constructed environments can start to approach extreme resolutions found in nature, both *in vitro* through simulation, and *in vivo* through automation and AI-enhanced construction. What could be called 'data materialisation' is opening up the potential for architecture to finally resonate with the complexity of ecology.

New design workflows necessitate explicit synthesis of big data from a multitude of sources. With such high information density, the new design problems are related to training and learning. They are problems of simulation. How can AI enhance human perception and creativity within these near-infinite data-rich design environments? The answer might be germinating already in the workflows of computational architecture, where the process of design becomes a process of searching for potential designs. Instead of drawing or modelling singular formal outcomes, design is happening at the convergence of AI-enabled pattern recognition and human-driven intent and decision making. A new frontier of creativity is emerging at this threshold between humans and machines that is becoming increasingly attuned to new sensibilities afforded by the machinic paradigm, and machines that are becoming increasingly organic. We are discovering new ways of seeing. Machines can see patterns that are invisible to humans, rendering the previously invisible visible.

The *Cloud Pergola* installation in the Croatian National Pavilion at the 2018 Venice Architecture Biennale emerged out of a lineage of research projects (such as Biothing and Wonderlab, 2012–17) on robotically 3D-printed lattice structures. It belongs to a family of proto-structures that are information packed, unprecedentedly intricate, lightweight yet strong and resilient. A multi-agent system algorithm was used to address particular goals driven by design intent and the specific constraints of the fabrication.

Three ascending swarms spin in counter directions to each other, resulting in a stronger and more balanced structure. This spinning behaviour leaves an aesthetic imprint on the lattice, with its diagonal struts shifting directionality, capturing this upward 'swarming'. At a certain height this behaviour changes, radically slowing down in the z direction to privilege horizontal movement, resulting in a ceiling sequence.

The structure is conceived as a mass rather than a geometry. It is not optimised, but finds its strength in very large numbers. Vectorial storms redirecting in counter-twists hold the high-resolution structural network together. Inspired by cloud formations and weather events, this mathematised cloud plays with the visitor's perception. Movement through the structure generates a series of dynamic interference views through its deep fabric, drifts and ruptures in visibility. A sea of redirecting vectors attracts the visitor like an invisible gravity force.

Even when 3D-printed in a 'proxy material' such as recyclable polymers, the strength of the *Cloud Pergola* structure is significant, achieved through a highly distributed large number of connections. These information-rich tectonics could deliver a myriad of potential advantages over our current incredibly heavy buildings with high CO_2 emissions, such as faster construction, less material, a high degree of heterogeneity and context sensitivity, and lightness.

AI in a form of supervised deep learning is used to train the robot to recognise what the node is and adapt in real time to the noise in material behaviour and accumulation of tolerances. This enables path regeneration, real-time visual tracking of material, and recomputing of robotic targets, thus increasing the resilience, speed and accuracy of robotic 3D printing.

An Ai-based field simulation from below. Machines can see patterns that are invisible to humans and render the previously invisible visible. The initial *Cloud Pergola* structures had a resolution of half a million voxels.

Alisa Andrasek with Madalin Gheorghe
and Bruno Juričić,
Cloud Pergola,
Croatian National Pavilion,
Venice Architecture Biennale,
2018

Developed in close collaboration with Arup engineers and robotic fabrication company Ai Build, the structure is conceived as a mass rather than geometry. It does not optimise, but finds its strength through the redundancy of a very large number of connections. Can we build data-rich architectures with fewer resources and CO_2 emissions?

Final blueprint of the structure printed for the Venice Biennale, optimised for the available robotic printing time by reducing the resolution from 500,000 to 40,000 voxels.

Damjan Jovanovic and Lidija Kljakovic

Dream Estate

Dream Estate is a self-driven, narrative real-time simulation set within a synthetic landscape populated with procedurally generated androids.[1] A simulation is an emerging narrative format that is defined by potentially endless, unscripted and unexpected variations and outcomes – a video game that plays itself.[2] The project explores the possibilities of procedural design for artificial humanoid agents, and focuses on the potential of these interconnected systems to enable and promote emergent storytelling.

A 'persona' is an elusive term that can be understood as an emergent property of numerous layers of an agent's behaviour system and their effect on an observer, first expressed through the agent's physical appearance, the complexity and shape of its body, movements and personality. The interplay between the agent's ability to evoke emotions and the observer's own propensity for pattern recognition and pareidolia is at the core of the 'agent-observer loop' positioned at the centre of Dream Estate's experiential potential. This loop is dependent on a fuzzy boundary between the appearance of intelligence and empathy and the emergence of actual emphatic behavioural patterns.

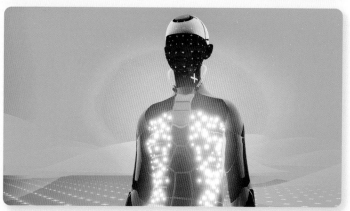

Grafting Minds

The project draws its conceptual stance from two positions found in the history of psychology: the Heider and Simmel 1944 study of apparent behaviour,[3] and Robert Plutchik's work in the 1980s on the nature and mapping of emotions.[4] Plutchik's work is interpreted as a blueprint for designing the depth of an agent's behaviour, which informs the multiple loops of interaction between agents and the world. The Heider and Simmel study motivates and informs the interaction loop between the simulation and the player-observer and frames the possible reading of the project as related to the natural propensity of the human mind to 'grant minds' to abstract objects.

top: Three autonomous agents sharing the space in the simulation.

middle: A procedural agent in a synthetic landscape.

right: Each agent's emotional state is expressed as a unique collection of symbols.

lifeforms.io (Damjan Jovanovic and Lidija Kljakovic),
Dream Estate,
2021

above: An agent communicates
through colour and light signals.

The development of the agents begins through the design of their emotional states and environmental influences. The project layers multiple variations of AI (behaviour trees and the open-source Generative Pre-trained Transformer 2 (GPT-2) created by OpenAI). The behaviour tree works like a brain, holding behaviour models that are further transferred to the AI non-player-character, controlling its body. At the start of the simulation, the androids have knowledge about just one emotion, but by interacting and exploring the world they exchange stories. The GPT-2 model is used to make the narrative they share, and each emotional state is expressed through a text generated by learning from a collection of texts by select philosophers and writers. The androids also develop a spatial relationship with their environment through the computationally defined environmental query system that maps and evaluates spatial details like obstacles, measuring distance, visibility and direction.

The goal of the project is to explore the storytelling potential and agency of artificial agents through activating and manipulating the observer's own 'theory of the mind' – their ability to grant thoughts, motivations, desires and intentions to others.

Notes
1. https://www.youtube.com/watch?v=-c9hmoHokl4
2. For a better understanding of this term see Ian Cheng, *Emissaries Guide To Worlding*, Serpentine Gallery and Koenig Books (London), 2018, and Damjan Jovanovic, 'Screen Space, Real Time', *Monumental Wastelands Magazine*, December 2021, pp 112–29.
3. Fritz Heider and Marianne Simmel, 'An Experimental Study of Apparent Behavior', *American Journal of Psychology* 57 (2), April 1944, pp 243–59.
4. Robert Plutchik, 'A General Psychoevolutionary Theory of Emotion', in Robert Plutchik and Henry Kellerman (eds), *Emotion: Theory, Research and Experience, Volume 1: Theories of Emotion*, Academic Press (New York), 1980, pp 3–33.

The Dragonfly Wing Project

Hao Zheng and Masoud Akbarzadeh

Nature has always been the master of design skills to which humans only aspire, but new approaches bring that aspiration closer to our reach than ever before.

Through 4.5 billion years of iterations, nature has shown us its extraordinary craftsmanship, breeding a variety of species whose body structures have gradually evolved to adapt to natural phenomena and make full use of their unique characteristics. The dragonfly wing, among body structures, is an extreme example of efficient use of materials and minimal weight while remaining strong enough to withstand the tremendous forces of flight. It has long been the object of scientific research examining its structural advantages to apply their principles to fabricated designs.[1] We can imitate its form and create duplicates, but thoroughly understanding the dragonfly wing's mechanism, behaviour and design logics is no trivial task.

Deciphering Nature

Among recently developed AI approaches, two that had not previously been used to analyse the geometric formation of this natural structure offered intriguing possibilities: a geometry-based equilibrium method called graphic statics for structural analysis; and machine learning for rule summarisation. To explore these possibilities, the Dragonfly Wing Project at the University of Pennsylvania's Polyhedral Structures Laboratory has used graphic statics to analyse the structural features of the convex-only networks of a dragonfly wing, and created a related dataset for machine learning.

The dataset contains the morphological form and topological force diagrams of dragonfly wings as images, and represents the corresponding edge lengths as vectors. It then trains the machine-learning model, which maps the connections between the morphology of the wing and the structural topology of its convex-only network. From this mapping, the trained machine-learning model can generate similar internal structures for any given morphological boundary.

After successfully learning the features of the dragonfly wing, the same method was applied to analyse structures from other species, including grasshopper wings, damselfly wings and Amazon water lilies. Surprisingly, the project shows that graphic statics provides the necessary features to analyse all of these lightweight structures, and the resulting data can be used to train machine-learning models. Not only does this method generate structural geometries similar to the original species, but it also successfully predicts the thickness of the bodily structures.

Trained by Nature

The results enable application of the design logic of a dragonfly wing to an efficient design method for other manufactured structures with similar performance needs; for example, the internal structure of an aeroplane wing. Using the boundary of a conventional aeroplane wing, the new approach can generate an internal structure based on the machine-learning training model of the dragonfly wing. The generated structure can then serve as an internal lightweight structure for an aeroplane wing, bringing the design logic of a highly efficient dragonfly wing to human-designed aircraft. Although the mechanical behaviour of this kind of generated structure calls for further research, multiple other varieties of architectural structures can be generated using this method.

The Dragonfly Wing Project opens a door to other related investigations, where training machine-learning models based on datasets derived from natural species can transfer design knowledge from nature to similar human structures. This approach may improve our understanding of various design parameters needed to craft human-made systems dealing with similar boundary conditions and enhance the performance of human designs.[2]

Notes
1. See Praveena Nair Sivasankaran *et al*, 'Static Strength Analysis of Dragonfly Inspired Wings for Biomimetic Micro Aerial Vehicles', *Chinese Journal of Aeronautics* 29 (2), 2016, pp 411–23, and Yunluo Yu *et al*, 'A Dragonfly Wing Inspired Biomimetic Aerodynamic Thrust Bearing for Increased Load Capacity', *International Journal of Mechanical Sciences* 176, 15 June 2020, 105550.
2. See Hao Zheng, Vahid Moosavi and Masoud Akbarzadeh, 'Machine Learning Assisted Evaluations in Structural Design and Construction', *Automation in Construction* 119, November 2020, 103346, and Hao Zheng and Philip F Yuan, 'A Generative Architectural and Urban Design Method Through Artificial Neural Networks', *Building and Environment* 205, November 2021, 108178.

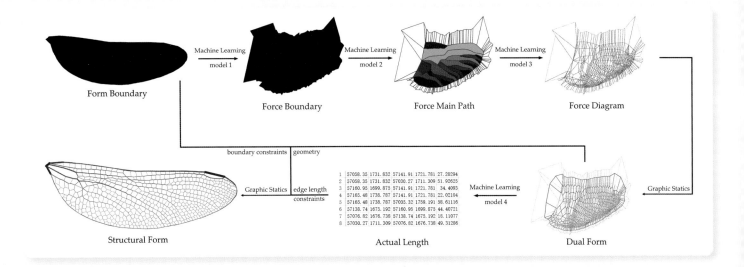

Form Boundary

Machine Learning model 1

Force Boundary

Machine Learning model 2

Force Main Path

Machine Learning model 3

Force Diagram

boundary constraints | geometry

Graphic Statics | edge length constraints

Actual Length

1	57058.35	1731.832	57141.91	1721.781	27.20294
2	57058.35	1731.832	57030.27	1711.309	51.92825
3	57160.95	1699.875	57141.91	1721.781	34.4093
4	57165.48	1738.787	57141.91	1721.781	22.02104
5	57165.48	1738.787	57035.32	1759.191	58.61116
6	57138.74	1675.192	57160.95	1699.875	44.40721
7	57076.82	1676.738	57138.74	1675.192	18.11077
8	57030.27	1711.309	57076.82	1676.738	49.31286

Machine Learning model 4

Graphic Statics

Structural Form

Dual Form

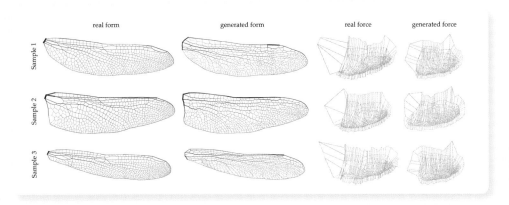

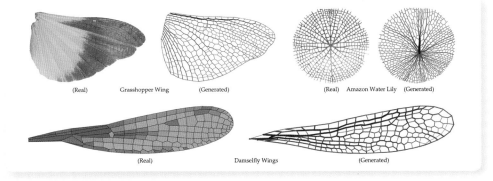

Hao Zheng / Polyhedral Structures Laboratory,
The Dragonfly Wing Project,
Stuart Weitzman School of Design,
University of Pennsylvania,
Philadelphia,
2021-

first: The workflow generates the structural form from its boundary using machine-learning models trained with design data from nature – for example, dragonfly wings – and the graphic statics method for the transformation between the geometry and the topology of the structure.

second: The generated structures are highly similar to real dragonfly wing structures.

third: Using the same workflow, the project trained three different machine-learning models with datasets of grasshopper wings, Amazon water lilies and damselfly wings. The image compares the real and generated structures.

fourth: By inputting the boundary of an aeroplane wing, the new method can generate the interior structure through the machine-learning models trained on dragonfly wing datasets. The image shows a prospective design scenario for this AI-assisted workflow.

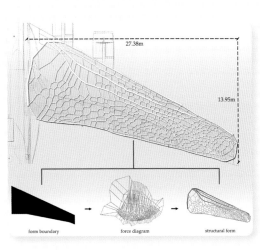

Artificial Relief

Kyle Steinfeld

We train our models, and thereafter our models train us.

Periods of technological change bring into stark relief the dynamic between the inherent affordances of design tools and the perceived autonomies of design practice. As machine-learning processes are introduced into computer-aided architectural design, the modes of action afforded by this new media will catalyse changes in the way we design. The Artificial Relief project, samples of which are shown here, represents an early probe into the nature of changes that machine-augmented architectural design might bring. It asks: What novel subjectivities might we embrace in this new medium, and what fresh liberties does it engender? Conversely, which of these new capacities should designers avoid, and what are the important domains of action that are denied?

In any semi-automated design process that produces an abundance of design candidates – generative design, for example – classification and selection are important authorial positions to hold. Machine augmentation is distinct from these earlier approaches. Here, an entirely new locus of authorship is offered the designer who trains, rather than constructs, their machine partner. This new locus is the dataset.

Designing through a dataset feels different from, for example, chaining together the series of mathematical and geometric operations that comprise a parametric model and other classical forms of computation. Why is this? For one thing, classical computation enforces orderliness, while datasets are often messy. They are at times so disordered that the particularly inconsistent and fragmented samples drawn from the real world are termed as originating 'in the wild'. This messiness affords acts of abduction: by playing with loosely structured combinations of unlike forms, our models help us connect unrelated ideas, thereby instrumentalising an approach to invention that has long been a mainstay of creative thought.

Further, while classical computation requires explicitness, datasets may be more ambiguous. They are collections of implicitly related examples, typically free from expressly defined relationships. This ambiguity affords tacit knowledge-in-action: we may make design moves that are less reliant on knowing precisely how to achieve them, and are more akin to saying that something should be 'more like this' or 'more like that'.

Finally, where classical computation feigns universality and objectivity, datasets are widely understood as artefacts of culture. They are incontestably historical records of past decisions and forms, and are inextricably embedded with the biases of those who author them. The fact that data is a part of material culture affords acts of curation: we may select those aspects of the past that we wish to hold influence on our future designs.

The Artificial Relief project stands as an illustration that the dataset is a key point of intervention in a machine-augmented process, and that data is the central material of this new medium. It displays forms that inhabit the boundary between the unrecognisable and the familiar, extrapolated from a dataset of fragmented Greco-Roman sculptural reliefs. Among the samples represented are those drawn from a Greek construction, the Pergamon Altar (2nd century BC), which was disassembled in the late 19th century and then reassembled in the early 20th century in a Berlin museum. Artificial Relief operates similarly. A set of selected forms are fragmented and described as deformations from a base plane. While machine-learning processes typically struggle to account for 3D forms, vector displacement maps such as these are comprehensible to the machine, and are employed to train a neural network to understand the form language of the selected source material. In classical computational style, our machine partner then generates an abundance of design candidates that adhere to this form language – a garden that bore the fruit seen here. ᴅ

Kyle Steinfeld, Titus Ebbecke, Georgios Grigoriadis and David Zhou, Two Charites, Artificial Relief, University of California, Berkeley, 2021

A machine-generated sculptural work that agglomerates multiple samples drawn from the latent space of a GAN trained on Greco-Roman sculptural forms. The piece takes its name from Greek mythology: the Charites are a group of sister goddesses who represent beauty, fertility and human creativity.

Kyle Steinfeld, Titus Ebbecke,
Georgios Grigoriadis,
and David Zhou,
Artificial Alto-Releivo,
Artificial Relief,
University of California,
Berkeley,
2021

Machine augmentation suggests a host of
possible material strategies – a number of ways
that a human author might wield a generative
adversarial network (GAN) to compose
ornamental form. One such compositional
strategy is demonstrated here. Recalling the
rhythmic symmetry of frieze patterns found in
traditional Western ornament, a 'walk' through
the latent space of a GAN trained on Greco-
Roman sculptural forms is aggregated across
a surface in high relief.

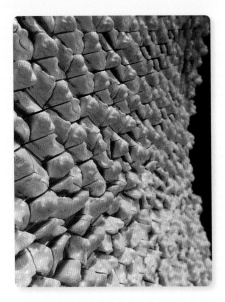

Kyle Steinfeld, Titus Ebbecke,
Georgios Grigoriadis and David Zhou,
A Pipeline for Representing
3D Sculptural Relief as Raster Data,
Artificial Relief,
University of California, Berkeley,
2021

A pipeline is developed for representing 3D polygon
meshes as 2D vector displacement maps. Given
a sample form (1), a fragment (2) is selected and
'squashed' onto a plane, with displacements between
points on the plane and locations on the 3D mesh
stored as vectors separated into their x, y and z
components (3). This vector information is stored as
the RGB channels of a raster image (4), a format that is
both amenable to a GAN and is able to be reinterpreted
as vector displacements from a base raster plane (5)
to reproduce similar sculptural forms (6).

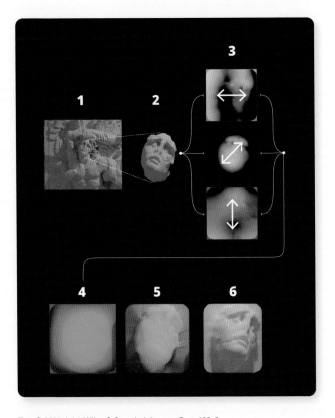

Kyle Steinfeld, Titus Ebbecke,
Georgios Grigoriadis and David Zhou,
A Synthetic Sculptural Form, Artificial Relief,
University of California, Berkeley,
2021

To highlight the unworked material produced by a GAN trained on
Greco-Roman sculptural forms, a synthetic form is extruded from its
base raster plane.

A Word from
∆D Editor
Neil Spiller

Architectural Intelligence

Colloquy of Mobiles Redux

Colloquy of Mobiles created a human environment that contains conversational machines, a condition that is now part of everyday life. While this was not broadly obvious in 1968, Pask saw it and created an example of it in *Colloquy*. This perhaps is its fundamental contribution.

Andrew Gordon Speedie Pask (1928–96) was a founding father of second-order cybernetics and the creator of 'conversation theory'. Conversation theory aims to be a comprehensive, rigorous scientific theory of any and all kinds of interactions, between any and all kinds of entities, whether biological, mechanical, electronic, linguistic or social. *Colloquy of Mobiles* was designed by Pask to illustrate some aspects of conversation theory. An early example of interactive architecture, it was made as part of the seminal 'Cybernetic Serendipity' exhibition at London's Institute of Contemporary Arts (ICA) in 1968. In 2018, to celebrate its 50th anniversary, *Colloquy* was made again, as a touring installation/exhibition, with a collaboration between Paul Pangaro, currently Professor of Practice in the Human-Computer Interaction Institute at Pittsburgh's Carnegie Mellon University and President of the American Society for Cybernetics, and Thomas J McLeish, MIT Media Lab graduate and independent researcher into interactive design and ubiquitous computing. Pangaro remembers meeting Pask as part of the MIT Architecture Machine Group under Nicholas Negroponte (later co-founder of the Media Lab and its first Director) in 1976. 'The lab benefitted from just the potency of having Pask around to respond to projects on the fly. I was immediately seduced by Pask's presence and by his ideas.'[1]

'Cybernetic Serendipity', curated by Jasia Reichardt, was decidedly an interdisciplinary curatorial project. McLeish states his appreciation of the diversity and multivalence of the exhibition's contributors. 'It was an incredible snapshot of a moment in history when huge leaps in technological capability were being passionately and creatively explored by wide fields of expertise. Like swimming the molten landscape of the earth before it hardened into less malleable crusts.' *Colloquy* was by far the most outrageous as well as important and far-seeing work in the whole exhibition. It looked as if it had fallen from outer space and yet reproduced interactions of competition and cooperation, all in the guise of a conversation between male and female forms that had 'drives' and behaved autonomously, not even needing the intervention of humans to operate fully.

Pask had a prescient vision of our future with machines that may choose to act on their own. *Colloquy* explores the nature of machine-to-machine and person-to-machine conversations in an immersive environment, which was the first of its kind. It has subsequently influenced generations of artists and critics concerned with the role of technology in everyday life. Pangaro describes its aims and objectives: 'It's clear that *Colloquy* has so much to say to our digital world, its limitations and its ability to contrast what we take for granted every day in our environment by way of computers and devices in our pockets and sensors on the Internet and all, with what it means to be analogue and nondeterministic and yes serendipitous. *Colloquy*, then and now, explores the dynamics of conversational

Gordon Pask, *Colloquy of Mobiles*, 'Cybernetic Serendipity' exhibition, Institute of Contemporary Arts (ICA), London, 1968

Gordon Pask in front of the male elements of *Colloquy*. Conversation theory, theorised by Pask, is a cybernetic theory whose generality and explanatory power – from understanding human-to-human dynamics to writing code – cyberneticist Paul Pangaro believes is unparalleled.

machines that now surround us every day, the impact of smart environments, which increasingly affect our lives and the implications of artificial intelligence, inside of every digital device we use.'

A Machinic Cocktail Party

Colloquy of Mobiles – in both of its manifestations – explores conversation theory through a loose metaphor of a cocktail party. We watch and can interact with two distinct sets of entities attempting to converse with each other in mutual feedback loops to reach individual states of contentment. The entities have contentment goals attained by transmitting and sharing light and sound in time. Unlike the tidy confines of a self-contained computer, the entities are attempting to communicate in a room amongst the background noise of ever-changing ambient light, reflections and unexpected light sources; sounds generated outside of the system by people and other machines; and slight mechanical disturbances caused by their motion in space. Much as today's

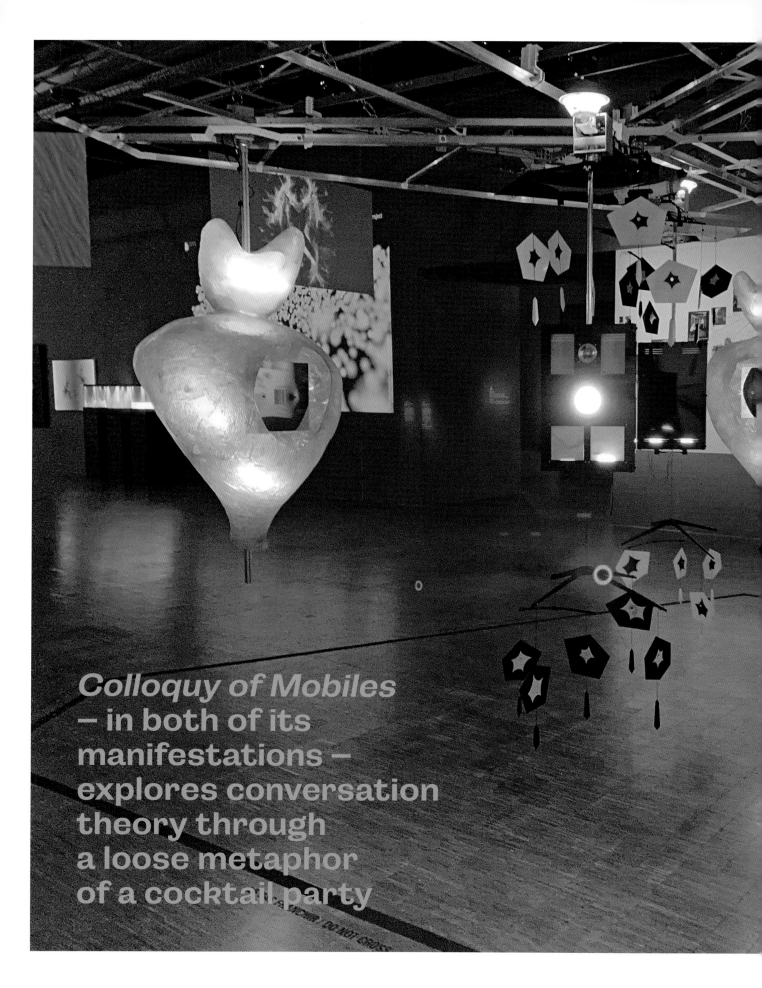

*Colloquy of Mobiles
– in both of its
manifestations –
explores conversation
theory through
a loose metaphor
of a cocktail party*

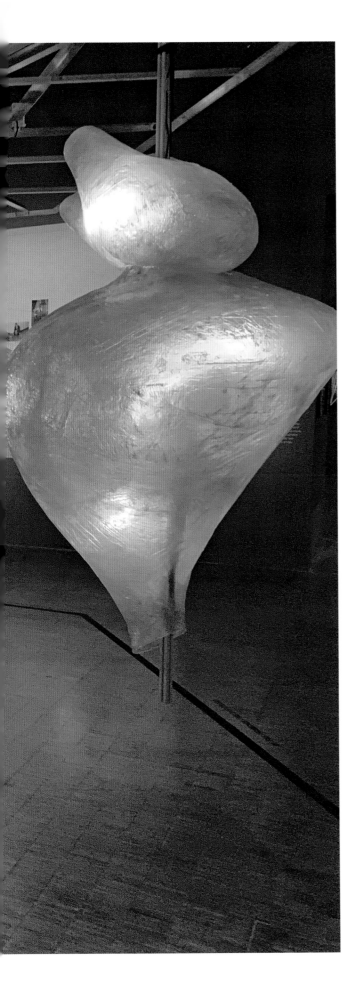

chatbot can impersonate a human, in *Colloquy* a human can impersonate one of the entities by communicating with the others in a way that closely mimics expected patterns of communication in light and sound.

Specifically, male and female figures rotate vertically back and forth on their own axes. Males are mounted at the end of a rotating bar so they also move through the interior space of the work while females hang from a fixed position. Males are sending out a signal of interest by flashing a large light in their centre. If this light falls upon a female, and she is interested in the offer, then she stops rotating, signals her interest via a sound pattern (that matches the flashing light pattern of the male) and flaps her mirror. If the male hears the signal, he orients himself in front of the female and keeps his light on steadily. As a result of this juxtaposition, the male's light hits the female's flapping mirror and reflects back to the male's sensors at the top and bottom of the male's form, which accumulates over time to 'satisfy his drive'. Simultaneously, the female's 'drive is being satisfied' by the continually shining light from the male. This continues until the female reaches a point of satisfaction and displays a brief light show to indicate this. Similarly the male reaches satisfaction (and in the original, made a sound described as 'hooting' like a car horn). We know from comments by Pask himself as well as written remarks by his collaborators that the analogy to sexual climax was intended and unmistakable. Once satisfied, each mobile returned to its earlier configuration of rotating and scanning for serendipitous interaction and possibly cooperation, through to satisfaction.

It is this sexual analogy that reminds one of Marcel Duchamp's biomechanical *The Bride Stripped Bare by Her Bachelors, Even* (1915–23) with its two domains of male and female setting up an electromagnetic essay in delay and desire. Pangaro comments on the male and female constitution of the mobiles: 'I've often felt it afforded an opportunity for satire, to stereotype males and females in the ritual of courtship, where the ego of the male (the light) was used to attract the female, whose mirror would feed the male's ego by reflecting back to the male.' McLeish offers a further observation: 'The male forms tend to be more "hunter"

Paul Pangaro and Thomas J McLeish,
Colloquy of Mobiles 2018,
College of Creative Studies,
Detroit, Michigan,
2018

As 2018 was the 50th anniversary of the original, the idea was to build a full-scale working replica and this generated a powerful momentum – as well as a sense of urgency. The team had little more than a year if they were to finish on time. After its initial tour, the installation entered the collection of the ZKM in Karlsruhe, Germany, which intends to continue to display it and share it with other institutions.

and the female forms more "gatherer". The male form is constantly calling out to the world [via light] looking for a partner, the female form is constantly listening for a partner that shares an interest. The male form wants to hear [see] what he transmits to the world transmitted back to him, the female form patiently endures being a repeater of what she hears [sees] … Another aspect is that gallery-goers can engage with the mobile elements using flashlights and thus enter the "conversation" that Pask had set up among the mobiles. By pretending to be mobiles, they distracted and interacted with the mobiles, who couldn't know whether they were interacting with other mobiles or humans.'

Colloquy of Mobiles 2018 was fabricated from November 2017. McLeish recounts its remaking: 'In Detroit we worked with the faculty and students of the College for Creative Studies to interpret the sparse original documentation of the physical piece and mobile-to-mobile interaction. The bulk of the fabrication took place in Chicago at mHUB. In Paris we worked with the amazing team at the Centre Pompidou to realise an instantiation that met the specific physical and electrical constraints of their space. We are currently working with ZKM in Karlsruhe (who are taking it into their collection) to make sure the piece can be easily supported and shared with other institutions.' ZKM is uniquely suited to maintain the work indefinitely (they have substantial staff dedicated to keeping the installations working).

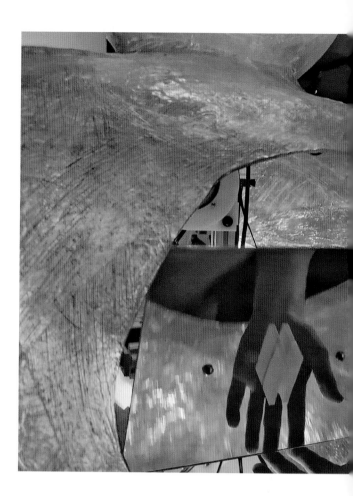

McLeish calibrating one of the female mirrors. The team expected there to be better and more complete documentation of the original work. They learnt an appreciation for the level of effort that must have gone into the original piece, bearing in mind the technologies available in 1968. Pask and his team had to invent not only the method of implementing the concept but also how to communicate with a team building it in hardware, software and form.

The Artificiality of AI

Grounded in how digital machines work, AI does its best to rise up to the level of interactivity that humans need, want and deserve, but it fails miserably. The entire digital culture is misguided: from how the logic works, to how software is designed and built, to the biases that suffuse the outcomes, to its service towards mercenary ends. The result at every step is so far away from what it means to be human, from what is required to nourish our analogue and biological beings. So humans are misused by so many applications of AI (social media, political polarisation, racist jurisprudence, to name a few).

Pangaro's critique of AI starts by analysing how AI embodies the meaning of interaction, information and intelligence. His thesis is that the problems caused by today's AI stem from these meanings. If we were to look at the same concepts from a cybernetic lens, he believes we would have much better, more humane relationships with our machines. McLeish notes there seems to be a great divide between the myth and mystery of AI and the real-world development and application of AI. Bridging this gap will require a richer understanding of how and what AI learns and when and where it uses what it has learnt on the part of those who will be designing the touchpoints of the world we build for ourselves.

Pangaro and McLeish want the *Colloquy 2018* project to change how we feel about interacting with machines. There has been little public debate about the societal and ethical questions presented to designers of these systems. *Colloquy 2018* will provoke designers of software, devices, products and services, across a wide spectrum of industries impacting all aspects of our daily life, to imagine and to debate the opportunities and challenges of pervasive, conversational machines.

The goals of *Colloquy of Mobiles* as an exploration are still valid and worthy of development even today. Pangaro and McLeish hope that their efforts at exhibition, experience/interaction and pedagogy will encourage others to continue to work with the cybernetic concepts and evolve a more humane approach to design, technology and AI.

We know from comments by Pask himself as well as written remarks by his collaborators that the analogy to sexual climax was intended and unmistakable

Note
1. All quotes from Paul Pangaro and Thomas J McLeish are from an email interview with Neil Spiller during July 2021.

Pangaro and McLeish assembling the installation. Given the cohort Pangaro brought together as a programming and fabrication team and the desire and will to see the piece recreated, there was incredible serendipity about reanimating the piece on its 50th anniversary. It was a question of the right people at the right time, an incredible opportunity.

Masoud Akbarzadeh is a designer with a unique academic background and experience in architectural design, computation and structural engineering. He is an assistant professor at the Weitzman School of Design, University of Pennsylvania, and the Director of the Polyhedral Structures Laboratory (PSL). He holds a Doctor of Science from the Institute of Technology in Architecture, ETH Zurich, where he was a research assistant in the Block Research Group. His main research topic is three-dimensional graphical statics, a novel geometric method of structural design.

Refik Anadol is a media artist, pioneer in the aesthetics of data and machine intelligence, and the director of Refik Anadol Studio in Los Angeles. He earned a BA degree in photography and video and an MA in visual communication design from Istanbul Bilgi University. He is also a lecturer and researcher for the University of California, Los Angeles (UCLA) Department of Design Media Art, where he obtained his Master of Fine Arts. Locating creativity at the intersection of humans and machines, he takes the data that flows around us as the primary material, and the neural network of a computerised mind as a collaborator.

Alisa Andrasek is Professor of Design Innovation at RMIT University in Melbourne, prior to which she directed a programme in advanced architectural design at the Bartlett School of Architecture, University College London (UCL). She is the founder of Biothing, a partner of Bloom Games, and co-founder of AI Build. Her work has been exhibited at the Centre Pompidou in Paris, the New Museum and Storefront for Art and Architecture in New York, FRAC Centre in Orléans, France, and at the Beijing, Sydney and Venice Biennales. She is currently working on bringing AI and robotics to the forefront of AEC industries.

Efilena Baseta is a co-founding partner of Noumena (Barcelona), a Senior Artist in the faculty of Architecture and Planning at the Vienna University of Technology, and a computational designer at Coop Himmelb(l)au. She is an architect engineer (National Technical University of Athens) and in 2019 completed her doctorate as a Marie-Curie Fellow at the University of Applied Arts Vienna. Her research interest lies in transformable structures using computational design and digital fabrication techniques with a strong material focus.

Daniel Bolojan is the founder of Nonstandardstudio, a PhD student at the University of Applied Arts Vienna, and an assistant professor at Florida Atlantic University's School of Architecture. His current study focuses on the development and application of deep-learning methodologies in architectural design, with a particular emphasis on issues of shared agency and the augmentation of the designer's creativity.

Shane Bugni is a teaching assistant for advanced fabrication, robotics and artificial intelligence in the Department of Architecture at Texas A&M University.

Alexandra Carlson is a PhD student at the Robotics Institute at the University of Michigan in Ann Arbor. She has served as a graduate student mentor for the Taubman College of Architecture and Urban Planning AI+Architecture Master's thesis studio for the past two years, and has collaborated on numerous architecture projects that involve modelling style in both images and 3D models. She has a BA in psychology from the University of Chicago, where she researched both computational neuroscience and physics.

Angelos Chronis is the head of the City Intelligence Lab at the Austrian Institute of Technology in Vienna, and teaches at the Institute for Advanced Architecture of Catalonia (IAAC) in Barcelona and the Bauhaus University in Weimar, Germany. He studied architecture at the University of Patras in Greece, and computational design at the Bartlett, UCL. He completed his PhD as a Marie-Curie Fellow at the Innochain Innovative Training Network. He has previously worked as an associate at Foster + Partners and has taught at the Bartlett, the IUAV in Venice and TU Graz.

Sofia Crespo is an artist and co-founder of Entangled Others Studio. She is interested in biology-inspired technologies, for example the way organic life uses artificial mechanisms to simulate itself and evolve, implying that technologies are a biased product of the organic life that created them and not a completely separate object. Her work explores the similarities between techniques of AI image formation, and the way that humans express themselves creatively, and cognitively recognise their world, bringing into question the potential of AI in artistic practice and its ability to reshape our understandings of creativity.

Gabriel Esquivel is an associate professor at Texas A&M University where he is currently the director of the T4T Lab and AI Advanced Research Lab. He received his Master of Architecture from the Ohio State University.

Behnaz Farahi trained as an architect, designer and critical maker based in Los Angeles. She holds a PhD in interdisciplinary media arts and practice from the University of Southern California (USC) School of Cinematic Arts. She is an assistant professor in the Department of Design at California State University in Long Beach. She explores how to foster an empathetic relationship between the human body and the space around it using computational systems. Her work addresses critical issues such as feminism, emotion, perception and

social interaction. She is the guest-editor (with Neil Leach) of △ *3D-Printed Body Architecture* (November/December, 2017).

Theodoros Galanos is a Senior Project Manager at the Austrian Institute of Technology. He works at the intersection of design and intelligence, and specialises in the development of advanced computational design technologies for the built environment that seek to generate, extract, collect and articulate design intelligence, innovative solutions that bring together disciplines and enable exploration and automation as driving factors of effective, efficient and creative design processes. His current work focuses on bespoke machine-learning workflows that produce meaningful and measurable outcomes across vast design spaces in a fraction of the time.

Eduard Haiman is a multidisciplinary designer working in urbanism, architecture, art and software engineering. In 2010 he founded Branch Point, the non-profit research and education initiative focused on the computational approach of architectural design. He is also a co-founder of the Mathrioshka digital art and R&D studio. He is a chief design officer, partner of Habidatum, and leads visualisation and user interfaces for big-data urban analysis. Most recently he has been focusing on using AI to rethink the notion of aesthetics and functionality in architecture.

Wanyu He is the founder and CEO of XKool Technology, co-founder of Future Architecture Lab, and a former senior project architect at OMA. She attained an MSc in architecture and urban design from the Berlage Institute at Delft University of Technology in the Netherlands. She is currently a Doctor of Design (DDes) candidate focusing on AI and architecture at Florida International University in Miami. She is an adjunct professor of the Master of Urban Design at the School of Architecture at the University of Hong Kong.

Jean Jaminet is an assistant professor at Kent State University College of Architecture and Environmental Design in Ohio. He holds a Master of Architecture from Princeton University in New Jersey, and a Bachelor of Science in architecture from Ohio State University.

Damjan Jovanovic is an architect, educator and game designer. He is a co-founder of the design studio lifeforms.io, and works as design faculty at SCI-Arc in Los Angeles. His work centres on the development of experimental software, and his interests lie in investigating the culture and aesthetics of software platforms, as well as questions of contemporary design education, authorship and creativity.

CONTRIBUTORS

Pelin Kivrak is Senior Researcher at Refik Anadol Studio and a scholar of comparative media studies. She holds a PhD in comparative literature from Yale University in New Haven, Connecticut, and a BA in literature from Harvard University in Cambridge, Massachusetts. Her academic research focuses on contemporary art and literature's engagement with philosophical and scientific genealogies of the concept of collective responsibility

Lidija Kljakovic is a Los Angeles-based digital artist and architect, and a co-founder of the transdisciplinary design studio lifeforms.io. Her interest lies in creating digital life forms, as well as using AI to simulate their behaviours and create unique personalities. She makes procedural tools for designing characters, architecture and fashion.

Immanuel Koh holds a joint assistant professorship in the Faculties of Architecture and Sustainable Design (ASD) and Design and Artificial Intelligence (DAI) at the Singapore University of Technology and Design (SUTD). He is also the recipient of the Hokkien Foundation Career Professorship. He obtained his PhD from the School of Computer Sciences and Institute of Architecture at the École polytechnique fédérale de Lausanne (EPFL) in Switzerland, and was nominated for the Best Thesis Prize and Lopez-Loreta Prize. Trained at the Architectural Association (AA) in London and at Zaha Hadid Architects, he now directs Artificial-Architecture at SUTD. He is the author of the book *Artificial & Architectural Intelligence in Design* (SUTD, 2020).

Maria Kuptsova is an artist, researcher and educator in the fields of transdisciplinary art and architecture who explores synthetic forms of intelligence and bio-machinic design techniques in her research and artistic practice. She is a PhD candidate and research associate at the Synthetic Landscape Lab, Institute of Urban Design, University of Innsbruck, as well as a senior lecturer at the ITMO University in Saint Petersburg.

Feileacan McCormick is a generative artist, researcher and former architect, and a co-founder of Entangled Others Studio. His practice focuses on ecology, nature and generative arts, with a focus on giving the more-than-human new forms of presence and life in the digital space.

Sandra Manninger is co-principal of SPAN, a practice that folds advanced design, culture and technology into one design ecology. Her work is in the collections of the FRAC Centre and Museum of Applied Arts (MAK), and has been published extensively. She is a pioneer of AI and architecture, collaborating with the Austrian Research Institute for Artificial Intelligence (OFAI) starting in 1996, and conducting workshops on machine learning in 2006 at the University of Applied Arts Vienna. She continues this research in

collaboration with Michigan Robotics as part of the Architecture + Artificial Intelligence Laboratory (AR²IL) at the Taubman College of Architecture and Urban Planning.

Lev Manovich is a Presidential Professor at The Graduate Center, City University of New York (CUNY), and a Director of the Cultural Analytics Lab. He is the author and editor of 14 books including *The Language of New Media* (MIT Press, 2001), *AI Aesthetics* (Strelka Press, 2018) and *Cultural Analytics* (MIT Press, 2020). He was included in the list of '25 People Shaping the Future of Design' in 2013 and the '50 Most Interesting People Building the Future' in 2014.

Achim Menges is a registered architect in Frankfurt and full professor at the University of Stuttgart where he is the founding director of the Institute for Computational Design and Construction (ICD) and the director of the Cluster of Excellence Integrative Computational Design and Construction for Architecture (IntCDC). In addition, he has been a visiting professor in architecture at Harvard University's Graduate School of Design (GSD) and held multiple other visiting professorships in Europe and the US. He graduated with honours from the AA School of Architecture.

Wolf dPrix is co-founder, CEO and design principal of Coop Himmelb(l)au, a studio globally recognised for its innovative and complex design approach at the intersection of architecture, art and technology. He is counted among the originators of the Deconstructivist architecture movement. Throughout his career, he has remained active in education and academic life. He has held teaching positions at the University of Applied Arts Vienna, AA, Harvard University, Massachusetts Institute of Technology (MIT), Columbia University, UCLA, Yale University, the University of Pennsylvania, SCI-Arc and other institutions around the world.

M Casey Rehm is a multidisciplinary designer and founding partner of Ishida Rehm Studio in Los Angeles. He teaches at SCI-Arc, where he is the coordinator of the Masters of Science in Architectural Technology post-professional programme. He received his BArch from Carnegie Mellon University in Pittsburgh, Pennsylvania, in 2005, and his Master of Science in Advanced Architectural Design from Columbia University in New York in 2009. His work focuses on the intersection of AI, data, digital media and design.

Karolin Schmidbaur is a professor at the Institute of Experimental Architecture, Building Construction and Technology at the University of Innsbruck, and Partner and Head of Research at Coop Himmelb(l)au. She holds a degree from the Technical University in Munich. Since 1992 she has been practising

internationally with Coop Himmelb(l)au in Austria, Mexico and the US, and has been active in teaching at international architecture schools. Her interest lies in design methodology and its implications for evolving building tectonics.

Neil Spiller is Editor of 𝔇, and was previously Hawksmoor Chair of Architecture and Landscape and Deputy Pro Vice Chancellor at the University of Greenwich, London. Prior to this he was Vice Dean at the Bartlett School of Architecture, UCL. He has made an international reputation as an architect, designer, artist, teacher, writer and polemicist. He is the founding director of the Advanced Virtual and Technological Architecture Research (AVATAR) group, which continues to push the boundaries of architectural design and discourse in the face of the impact of 21st-century technologies. Its current preoccupations include augmented and mixed realities and other metamorphic technologies.

Kyle Steinfeld is an architect who works with code. Through a hybrid practice of creative work, scholarly research and software development, he reveals overlooked capacities of computational design, finding no disharmony between the rational and whimsical, the analytical and uncanny, the lucid and bizarre. His work is expressed through a combination of visual and spatial material. Through these, he seeks to undermine the imperative voice so often bestowed upon the results of computational processes, and to express in its place a range of alternative voices.

Thomas Wortmann is a tenure-track professor of computing in architecture at the ICD, University of Stuttgart. He holds a Master in Architectural Design from the University of Kassel, a Master of Science in Design and Computation from MIT, and a PhD in architecture and sustainable design from SUTD. Before joining the ICD, he taught at the National University of Singapore and held a position at Xi'an Jiaotong-Liverpool University in Suzhou, China. He researches the use of computational methods such as optimisation, multivariate visualisation and machine learning in architectural design processes, and leads the development of Opossum, a machine-learning-based optimisation tool.

Hao Zheng is a PhD researcher at the Weitzman School of Design, University of Pennsylvania, specialising in machine learning, digital fabrication, mixed reality and generative design. He holds a Master of Architecture from the University of California, Berkeley, and Bachelor of Architecture and Arts degrees from Shanghai Jiao Tong University. He previously worked as a research assistant at Tsinghua University in Beijing and at the University of California, Berkeley, focusing on robotic assembly, machine learning and bio-inspired 3D printing.

What is *Architectural Design*?

Founded in 1930, *Architectural Design* (△) is an influential and prestigious publication. It combines the currency and topicality of a newsstand journal with the rigour and production qualities of a book. With an almost unrivalled reputation worldwide, it is consistently at the forefront of cultural thought and design.

Issues of △ are edited either by the journal Editor, Neil Spiller, or by an invited Guest-Editor. Renowned for being at the leading edge of design and new technologies, △ also covers themes as diverse as architectural history, the environment, interior design, landscape architecture and urban design.

Provocative and pioneering, △ inspires theoretical, creative and technological advances. It questions the outcome of technical innovations as well as the far-reaching social, cultural and environmental challenges that present themselves today.

For further information on △, subscriptions and purchasing single issues see:

https://onlinelibrary.wiley.com/journal/15542769

Volume 91 No 3
ISBN 978 1119 747222

Volume 91 No 4
ISBN 978 1119 717522

Volume 91 No 5
ISBN 978 1119 717706

Volume 91 No 6
ISBN 978 1119 812241

Volume 92 No 1
ISBN 978 1119 743255

Volume 92 No 2
ISBN 978 1119 748793

How to Subscribe
With 6 issues a year, you can subscribe to △ (either print, online or through the △ App for iPad)

Institutional subscription
£357 / US$666
online only

£373 / US$695
print only

£401 / US$748
print and online

Personal-rate subscription
£151 / US$236
print and iPad access

Student-rate subscription
£97 / US$151
print only

△ **App for iPad**
6-issue subscription:
£44.99 / US$64.99
Individual issue:
£9.99 / US$13.99

To subscribe to print or online
E: cs-journals@wiley.com
W: https://onlinelibrary.wiley.com/journal/15542769

Americas
E: cs-journals@wiley.com
T: +1 877 762 2974

Europe, Middle East and Africa
E: cs-journals@wiley.com
T: +44 (0) 1865 778315

Asia Pacific
E: cs-journals@wiley.com
T: +65 6511 8000

Japan (for Japanese-speaking support)
E: cs-japan@wiley.com
T: +65 6511 8010

Visit our Online Customer Help
available in 7 languages at www.wileycustomerhelp.com/ask